C000173873

CONTENTS

Rutland Parade looking towards Lower Morden Lane, 7 February 1955. The old pre-Second World War one-candle-power street lights are about to be decommissioned and replaced by the modern concrete sodium type, which are already in place but unlit. Sutton and Cheam already have the much brighter sodium lights, which accounts for the bright glare in Epsom Road in the distance. (© Alan Cross)

2·50

MERTON & MORDEN

PAST & PRESENT

SARA GOODWINS

SUTTON PUBLISHING

Sutton Publishing Limited
Phoenix Mill · Thrupp · Stroud
Gloucestershire · GL5 2BU

First published 2006

Copyright © Sara Goodwins, 2006

British Library Cataloguing in Publication Data
A catalogue record for this book is available from the
British Library.

ISBN 0-7509-4189-8
Typeset in 10.5/13.5 Photina.
Typesetting and origination by
Sutton Publishing Limited.
Printed and bound in England by
J.H. Haynes & Co. Ltd, Sparkford.

> *For past and present residents of the area, Alan Cross and Derek and Sue Poulter, without whose encouragement, enthusiasm and considerable help this book would not have been written.*

Title page photograph: Corner of London Road and Central Road, *c.* 1950. The water trough in the centre of the photograph was the gift of Miss Juliette Reckitt in 1906 'in memory of the horses that suffered in the South African War'. Miss Reckitt might have got the idea from the Metropolitan Drinking Fountain and Cattle Trough Association. Founded in 1859, it was first concerned only with providing good, clean drinking water for people, but added the cattle trough appellation in 1867 perhaps persuaded by the fact that the water was being consumed by both people and animals anyway. The water trough still exists, although not in its original position; it is now further up the road outside St Lawrence's Church (see page 84). (© *Alan Cross*)

Opposite page: 1 Litchfield Avenue, 12 February 1955. When new the house cost £1,050 – a considerable sum in 1955. Concrete roads were the norm at the time, but this particular Crouch development (Litchfield Avenue, Rustington Walk, Hartland Way, Rutland Drive, Wentworth Close and Amberley Way) had roads that were made of pink rather than white concrete. The year 1955 was particularly bad for snow. Freezing weather began in the first week of January, with snow showers and blizzards becoming the norm. The heaviest fall of snow in the Morden area was on 24 February, almost a fortnight after this picture was taken. (© *Alan Cross*)

INTRODUCTION

Today Merton and Morden are busy communities of roughly the same size. Both are within striking distance of London, both have seen major developments in the last century and both grew faster between the First and Second World Wars than almost any other part of Greater London. After the Second World War Merton and Morden Urban District Council became one of the largest in the country in terms of population. Yet historically they could not have been more different. Merton was colonised early. Merton Priory was not only a great religious house but also an alternative centre for Court and Parliament if flood, sickness or the King's whim took them from Westminster. Morden, on the other hand, remained a tiny hamlet even into the twentieth century.

There have been people living in the area since the Stone Age but the Catuvelauni tribe which was living in the area when the Romans invaded in AD 43 are the first we can name. Around AD 33 – historians argue about the exact date – the Romans built Stane Street, which runs south through Merton and Morden to Chichester and the coast. Stane Street is something of a poor relation as regards Roman roads. Nowhere near as well built as the Fosse Way or Ermine Street, it is generally believed to have been laid down in a hurry, but no one is sure whether it was primarily a military road or one used mainly by traders. The builders could not have been helped by the fact that the area was probably marshy. The name Merton comes from the Old English *mere* meaning water and *tūn* meaning a farmstead. Merton is therefore the farm by the water. Morden, too, comes from the Old English; *mōr* meaning marshland and *dūn* a hill. Morden is thus a hill in marshland.

The two towns are about 12 miles from London; just the right distance for a local staging post or *mansio*. Similar to the coaching inns of later centuries, *mansiones* provided travellers with shelter, a change of horses and a measure of protection. Settlements grew up round them, and local inhabitants would have traded home-grown food and locally-made goods for more exotic wares. Roman pottery, tiles and coins have been found as recently as 1994 when the Phipps Bridge estate was being redeveloped.

The area has long had royal connections, with Merton being mentioned in charters by Kings Eadred and Edgar, while Morden was royal property given to Westminster Abbey before the Norman conquest. Merton Priory gave even more prominence to the area; when Westminster flooded in 1236 the large priory buildings were used for a meeting of a great council – a sort of forerunner of Parliament. At that meeting the eleven Statutes of Merton were drawn up which still form an important cornerstone of the Common Law of England. The setting was appropriate; four years earlier Hubert de Burgh, a great justiciar, had fled to

Beverley Roundabout looking down Garth Road to the entrance to Battersea New Cemetery, 8 October 1957. The fields to the right were notorious for being waterlogged and flooding was common. Before the Second World War cows were walked down Lower Morden Lane to these fields from Peacock Farm. Burial grounds, as distinct from churchyards, were a Victorian development to solve the health problems caused by the severe overcrowding of London churchyards. Several London parishes established cemeteries outside the metropolis and the Battersea cemetery opened in 1891 on land purchased from Hobald's Farm. Today the cemetery is operated by Wandsworth Borough Council. It has been declared a site of metropolitan importance for nature conservation because of the variety of rare grasses and wildflowers it contains. (© *Alan Cross*)

sanctuary in Merton and only urgent appeals to King Henry III had prevented his sanctuary being violated and him hauled out by an angry mob.

After the dissolution of the monasteries Merton declined in glamour, but remained a very important industrial centre. The River Wandle was the source of motive power and mills have been built along its bank since before Domesday. Connolly's Mill has a sign high up on the wall which states: 'this building stands on, or close to, a site which has been used for milling for at least 750 years. The present building was erected by the eminent engineer John Rennie shortly before 1800. Then known as Merton Mill it was one of the largest corn mills in the London area at the time. The building was converted to provide housing in 1994.' The caption is a neat précis of eight centuries of Wandle mills.

If Merton is old, Morden is nouveau riche! At the beginning of the twentieth century only 960 people lived in Morden, which was acknowledged as one of the smallest of the ancient Surrey parishes. The preservation of its rural nature for so long is largely down to the Hatfeild family who purchased most of Morden at the end of the nineteenth century and so preserved it from the building that was overtaking its northern neighbour.

The area has been shaped by its past. The split channels of the Wandle in Morden Hall Park were created by millers constructing watercourses to conduct the water supply to their mills. Green Lane appears on some of the earliest maps of the area and is virtually unchanged. The course of the Surrey Iron Railway, the first public railway in the world, ran along Church Road. Merton and Morden's past is rich and varied; you only have to look for it.

1

A Tale of Two Towns

Cast-iron boundary marker for Morden Parish, corner of Canterbury Road and Pilgrim Close, 6 February 2005. The year 1882 saw the passing of the Divided Parishes Act. By it, parishes with separate outlying areas had those separate areas automatically transferred to the parishes in which they were situated geographically. There is nothing to show whether this marker was added to a 'new' part of Morden Parish or laid claim to an existing part, but the new Act possibly made ancient parishes nervous and inclined to claim their own. H. Knight was presumably a local worthy and responsible for erecting the boundary markers. *(George Hobbs)*

Linked geographically and politically, Merton and Morden are small towns each with its own distinctive character. Merton was once a place of considerable importance. The Domesday Book compiled in 1086 states: 'Meretone was assessed . . . at 20 hides. There is land for 21 ploughs. In demesne are 2 ploughs and 56 villeins and 13 bordars with 18 ploughs. There is a church and 2 mills rendering 6s and 10 acres of meadow and woodland for 80 swine.' A hide is the amount of land which would support a household, a plough often a measure of the amount of tax an area was expected to bear (like council tax). Villeins, bordars and cottars (see below) are all ranks of peasant and often associated with towns; only the heads of households or people with significant wealth in their own right were recorded in Domesday so each peasant numbered may well have had a wife and several children. The mills would have been watermills; the River Wandle has a history of mill use and windmills were not introduced to the country until almost a year after Domesday. Translated, Domesday says that Merton covered about 2,500 acres with possibly as many as 500 inhabitants in about 70 dwellings. Merton was both rich and, for the time, densely populated.

By contrast, Morden or 'Mordone' was much smaller: 'in demesne are 3 ploughs and 8 villeins and 5 cottars with 4 ploughs. There is 1 slave and a mill . . .' Slavery in its modern sense did exist in eleventh-century England but a slave was also a term for a landless villager, so presumably the slave mentioned here was the miller. Morden therefore consisted of about fourteen households with a total of perhaps fifty people.

Originally fairly extensive, Merton became even more important with the founding of the Augustinian Priory in 1115 by Gilbert, Sheriff of Surrey. A temporary timber monastery was built before the first stone of the new priory church was laid in 1130. Gilbert the Norman laid the first stone, Prior Robert the second, and each of the thirty-six brethren one in succession. So important did Merton Priory become that Henry III had private quarters there by 1258 and, a century later, royal sporting spectacles were held regularly in the area.

No book which includes Merton would be complete without some mention of Admiral Lord Nelson, arguably the town's most famous resident. Born to a parson in the village of Burnham Thorpe, Norfolk, Horatio Nelson was rewarded after his victory over the French at the Battle of the Nile with the title Baron Nelson of The Nile and Burnham Thorpe. He thus became Lord Nelson but, although titled, was by no means particularly rich. He, Lady Hamilton and her elderly husband Sir William had already formed what Emma called *tria iuncto in uno* ('three joined in one'). Nelson had never before owned property and wanted a place reasonably near London and Portsmouth where the three of them could live together. He also wanted land suitable for farming as he intended farming to be a source of income once he had left the Navy. Merton Place seemed ideal and Nelson bought it in 1801 for £9,000 plus an additional £1,000 for the furniture – it cost him almost all he had.

It was from Merton that Nelson set out for the battle of Trafalgar on 13 September 1805. Six weeks later he was dead. Merton Place was left to Lady Hamilton who lived in it for a further three years before being forced to sell to settle her debts. After standing empty for many years the estate was eventually auctioned as 'lots adequate for detached villas' at the White Hart, Merton at noon on 16 September 1823. It was demolished in 1846. The area is now covered with housing and an industrial estate. Only the name, Nelson's Fields, shows where the manor house and pleasure grounds once were.

The White Hart itself is one of Merton's two oldest pubs – the other is the Leather Bottle; both existed by 1700 – and for a time it acquired an unusual local nickname. On 20 June 1935 the landlord, Edward Macey, shot himself. A mere five months later on 24 November the barman, David Robbins, was found hanged. After the double suicide locals began referring to the White Hart as the 'Rope & Gun'. The pub also has another local claim to fame: it was once owned by William Rutlish, founder of Rutlish School.

Perhaps fittingly for a sailor whose body was brought home in a keg of brandy, Nelson and his lady are also honoured in several pubs around the area. There is the Trafalgar, the Emma Hamilton and, with unconscious irony, the Nelson Arms. This last is in Merton High Street and has magnificent exterior tiling showing a battle at sea. There are reputed to be more pubs named after Nelson than after any other individual but the Nelson Arms may claim a more direct connection with him. It was founded in 1829, although the current building dates back to 1910, and built close to the site of the lodge and carriage gates to Merton Place.

Other glimpses of the former stately home still exist in the area; one such is the public space next to St John's Church called the Nelson Gardens. On a stone between two cannon and surrounded by bushes, a plaque reads: 'As a memorial of Lord Nelson and the splendid services which he rendered to his country this land which formed part of his Merton Estate was given on the first centenary of his death to The Merton Parish Council for a public recreation ground by a Great Nephew of the late Rear Admiral, Isaac Smith of Merton Abbey'. Admiral Smith, who is buried in the churchyard of St Mary's, Merton Park, was related by marriage to Captain James Cook, the great naval explorer. The young Smith was reputed to be the first man from Cook's ship *Endeavour* to set foot in Australia when he obeyed his captain's orders to 'jump out, Isaac!'

Merton High Street is a curious mix of small individual shops on one side of the road and residential housing on the other. It must be one of the few high streets in Greater London that has a river running along one side of part of it. Computer spellcheckers sometimes change 'Morden' to 'modern', and recent developments make it indeed a much more modern town. Even in Morden there is a definite contrast between the remnants of old buildings, the larger housing (for larger families) and green spaces of the early twentieth century, and cramped new developments with minimal garden and car parking squashed into the available space.

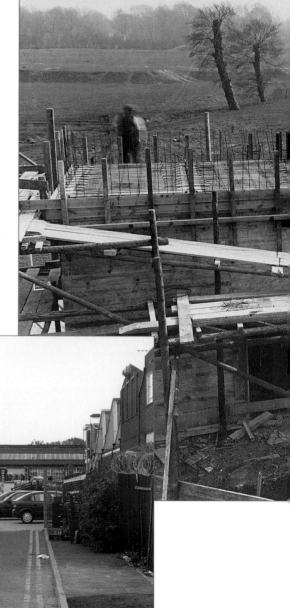

Unnamed access road off Deer Park Road, looking south, 11 June 2005. Merton Pumping Station is immediately to the photographer's right. Understandably, the roof of the waterworks was not accessible from which to take photographs, but it makes little difference. All of the open area visible in the photograph above is now covered by Merton Industrial Park. The building directly ahead is occupied by Pr Products, quality label manufacturers, while the one to the left is Circadia Bespoke Banqueting Fayre. *(George Hobbs)*

Building Merton Pumping Station and Works, 5 April 1933. Looking south, this view shows the roofing of the lime-mixing house where lime and coke were to be stored. Note that the scaffolding is made entirely of wood. The bank in the background on the left is all that remains of a calico-bleaching ground which was a series of parallel banks and ditches. Prepared calico was spread on the banks while 'whitsters' soaked the calico by scooping water from the ditches. While drying the cloth, the sun also bleached it. The whole process took about a month. Joseph Ancell's calico works was the first recorded in Merton in 1724 and was one of the factories leased by Edmund Littler (see page 122). *(Courtesy Sutton and East Surrey Water)*

Building Merton Pumping Station and Works, 4 July 1933. Looking west, Morden Road is visible in the distance. To the right the warehouses front onto the railway line. 'Hellesens dry batteries' advertises the wares of the largest manufacturer of dry batteries in Denmark. The foreground shows the reinforcement to the trusses and roof decking of the pumping station engine house. *(Courtesy Sutton and East Surrey Water)*

Merton Pumping Station and Works, 11 June 2005. The pitched roof being constructed in the upper photograph is just visible. The white building this side of it was built as a softening building and included the filter house and lime-mixing house. The water for Merton and Morden is now supplied from Cheam, which is one of nine treatment works. The Sutton and East Surrey Water company supplies water to 265,000 properties over 322 square miles. Merton is its most northerly supply area. *(George Hobbs)*

Merton High Street, *c.* 1910. The pub in the centre background was originally known as the Six Bells. It became the Royal Six Bells to advertise the fact that the Prince of Wales, later Edward VII, stopped here for refreshment on his way to the Epsom Derby. The steamroller to the right of the tram was made by Aveling & Porter Ltd. The logo on the front is a rearing horse with the word 'Invicta' on a scroll beneath it. Aveling & Porter were based in Rochester and made nearly 4,000 such roadrollers, which was almost two-thirds of the number made in Britain at the time. *(Author's collection)*

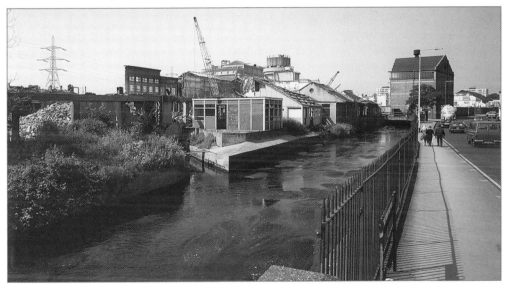

Demolition of DRG Board Mills, 1985. Bounded by the River Wandle on the west and the Pickle Ditch to the east, there has been a paper mill here since at least the beginning of the last century. First operated by Albert E. Reed, founder of Reed International, it became Merton Board Mills in 1923. During the 1940s and 1950s John Dickinson, a stationer based in Hemel Hempstead, opened or acquired several paper mills around the country, probably including Merton Board Mills. Certainly the Dickinson Robinson Group (DRG) was using it as a packaging works when it closed in about 1980. Recycling is not new; it was to this mill during the Second World War that local residents brought their waste paper for salvage. *(Courtesy The Sainsbury Archive)*

Building Merton Savacentre, 19 October 1987. This, the most southerly part of the site, was the first to be developed. Above the works and almost in the centre of the photograph is Liberty Mill, now called Merton Abbey Mills (see page 122). The photograph was taken from The Tower, built at the end of Collier's Wood High Street where it runs into Merton High Street. Once called 'Brown & Root House' when it was leased by that company, it is known by almost everyone locally as The Black Tower because it is covered with smoked glass. The best view of the area may be obtained from its windows – largely because, from them, you can't see The Tower itself. It's an eyesore! *(Courtesy The Sainsbury Archive)*

Water fountain, Miller's Mead Park, 6 August 2005. Because of tightened security, access wasn't available to The Tower to take photographs from its windows, but this, an older and much more elegant tower, is visible just down the road. Inscriptions on the memorial say: 'This ground and water opened to the public on July 11 1907, are vested in the National Trust for places of historic interest or natural beauty' and 'This garden is given for the enjoyment of the people of Wimbledon and Merton in memory of John Feeney of Birmingham and Berkswell one who loved nature and his fellow men.' Around the base of the memorial run the words: 'Calm Soul of All Things Make it mine to feel amid the City's Jar that there abides a peace of thine man did not make and cannot mar.' *(George Hobbs)*

Opening, Merton Savacentre, 28 February 1989. Savacentre brought together Sainsbury's fresh foods, groceries and toiletries, and British Home Stores' (BHS) clothing, household goods and lighting. The store had fifty newly-designed checkouts as well as special trolleys designed for wheelchair users and for mums with babies and young children. Fittingly, the two top men attended the opening. Standing are Sir Terence Conran (left), head of Storehouse which owns BHS, and David Sainsbury, Deputy Chairman of J. Sainsbury at the time. David became Baron Sainsbury of Turville in 1997. The Buckinghamshire village also has another claim to fame; it's where the BBC filmed the comedy programme *The Vicar of Dibley*. *(Courtesy The Sainsbury Archive)*

Merton Savacentre, 6 August 2005. Designed by Chapman Taylor Partners, the building was intended to be reminiscent of Crystal Palace. When it was opened it was the largest hypermarket in the UK covering an area the size of one-and-a-half football pitches. Appropriately, as Savacentre covers much of the site of Merton Priory, local clergyman the Revd Keith Uphill visited the hypermarket to bless the store, workers and shoppers. He also gave a talk on the area's historic past. Internationally renowned, the architects have worked on such projects as the Rostokino shopping centre in Moscow, opened in 1996, and Admiralty Basin, Tallinn, Estonia, opened in 1997. Currently Chapman Taylor is working on Terminal 5 at Heathrow Airport, which is due to be completed in 2008. *(George Hobbs)*

The Crown Inn, *c.* 1948–9. Historians claim that either the Crown or the Red Lion is the most common pub name and often indicate that a hostelry has existed for a long time. There has certainly been a Crown Inn in Morden since at least 1801; this is the third incarnation of the name, built in 1932. Note the police box and air raid sirens; the latter still existed in the 1960s. The photograph is believed to have been taken from the roof of the Odeon cinema. *(Courtesy Paul Hughes)*

Crown House, 22 May 2005. Designed by Arthur H. Shea, Crown House was built by Bernard Sunley & Sons and completed in 1961. As well as town hall and civic centre the complex includes shops and some commercial office space. Closest to the photographer is the library extension built in 1990. Bernard Sunley went on to design other municipal buildings until, in 1966, the firm became famous for a different reason. It was taken to court by East Ham Corporation for negligence when supervising the construction of a building. Today the case is often quoted as one which limits damages for a defective building to the cost of remedial work. *(George Hobbs)*

Morden Social Club, 17 April 1954. The social club was established by 1890 when most of Morden was owned by Gilliat Hatfeild. Mr Hatfeild assumed the traditional role of Lord of the Manor when he purchased Morden Hall in 1872. Who built the social club is not known but Mr Hatfeild did a great deal for local people, so the hall may well have been built and maintained at his expense. To modern eyes it looks very small, but the population of Morden was still under 1,000 when the club was established. Alma's Bakery, prominently displaying its advertisement for Hovis, always used to have a fine array of loaves on display. *(© Alan Cross)*

Crown Inn, 22 May 2005. The Crown Inn (see previous page) is now on the south-west corner of the triangle of roads formed by London Road, Crown Lane and Crown Road. The name is just visible above the chevrons and the traditional inn sign looks slightly incongruous on the stark frontage. As the photographer discovered, from certain angles the curve of Crown House makes it appear as though it's toppling over. Most worrying if you're standing underneath! Only fifty years separate these two photographs but buildings have proliferated, traffic has increased and instead of trees we have CCTV cameras. *(George Hobbs)*

Corner of London Road and Crown Road, 17 April 1954. Built about 1880, this terraced row was one of the earliest developments of artisans' houses in Morden and for many years looked out across houses and trees (see page 40). The newsagent also sold groceries and tea, etc. The sign above the entrance to the house about two doors down says E. Peto. It's difficult now to be sure but Morden did have a jobbing cobbler called E. Peto. Perhaps this was him? *(© Alan Cross)*

Corner of London Road and Crown Road, 11 June 2005. Road widening and traffic have prevented this photograph from being taken from exactly the same spot, but this, one of the earliest rows of cottages in Morden, still survives. Part of the old newsagent shop is now the headquarters of the Anthony Nolan Trust, the first and still one of the largest registers of bone marrow donors in the world. Started in 1971 by Shirley Nolan to find a donor for her son Anthony, the Trust now provides 400 donors for patients every year. Sadly the little boy died in 1978 without a donor being found in time. *(George Hobbs)*

The Holt, London Road, Remembrance Day, 1964. Don't be fooled by the late 1940s Ford as people expected to keep their vehicles for much longer then than they do now. Remember Green Shield Stamps? Between 1959 and 1964 trading stamps became a hugely popular way of passing on deferred discounts and thereby circumventing the resale price fixed by manufacturers. Green Shield Stamps were the Air Miles of the time. Powlesland Service Station, run by W.M. Palmer, is just off to the right. *(Courtesy 43F Squadron ATC)*

The Holt, London Road, 10 April 2005. Remarkably little has changed. The trees have gone and the garage no longer sells fuel but concentrates on second-hand cars. It also offers a personalised car wash with teams of young men descending on each vehicle. In the 1930s the *Morning Post* sports ground existed behind The Holt on this site. Presumably the area was once wooded as holt is an archaic word for a wooded hill, while Goodwood Close is in the background. *(George Hobbs)*

Hatherleigh, London Road, 8 October 1957. This was a substantial and elegant residence although the railway, which passes behind the trees to the left, is virtually on a level with the bedroom windows and passing trains must have been noisy. Originally the house had a semicircular drive, each end of which opened onto the London Road. The drive swept past the house to the right and led to an open carriage area to the rear. There was also a stable block, summer house and, apart from the conservatory, a large greenhouse. (© *Alan Cross*)

Hatherleigh seen in context, London Road, 8 October 1957. The house is about to be demolished to make way for 'new luxury maisonettes' to be sold by New Ideal Homesteads Ltd. Only the name remains: Hatherleigh Close is built on what was once the back garden. Frank R. Marchant is the surveyor; the firm still has offices further up London Road next to the Anthony Nolan Trust (see page 18). Just visible beyond the railway embankment buttress is a small gate which marks the entrance to a footpath leading to Merton Park. (© *Alan Cross*)

London Road, 11 June 2005. One of the most noticeable things about modern Morden is the expansion of its roads. Many which were once narrow and tree-lined are now dual carriageways (see page 84). Cycle lanes such as the one in the picture are intended to encourage the use of bicycles and thus reduce the number of cars on the road. Unfortunately most of the lanes are designed by car users who seem not to understand the skills of cycling. Consequently cycle lanes are often far too narrow and disappear at junctions. (*George Hobbs*)

Girder bridge over London Road, from the corner of Rosedene Avenue, 16 June 1954. Built by Horsley Ironworks of Tipton, the railway bridge spanned a much wider gap than the width of the carriageway at the time, which was fortunate as when the road was widened to a dual carriageway no alteration to the bridge was necessary. Horsley Ironworks was renowned for its bridges but also had another claim to fame. In 1822 it built the world's first iron steamship, the *Aaron Manby*, which spent most of its working life on the River Seine in France. (© *Alan Cross*)

Girder bridge over London Road, from the corner of Rosedene Avenue, 6 August 2005. The bridge is the only truss-girder bridge on the line, which means that the train travels through an iron framework rather than just over the top of supporting girders. It is made of 280 tons of steel and the main girders are 135ft long. The length of the bridge and the fact that it was built on a fairly sharp bend in the road are the reasons why truss-girder construction was used. The pillar box in the upper photograph has been removed because the building on the right is a Royal Mail sorting office; letters may now be posted in a box in its wall. (*George Hobbs*)

London Road, looking east, early 1954. In the background is a rare uninterrupted view of Morden South station. The station was opened on 5 January 1930 and soon proved very popular, increasing its sales of tickets five-fold in the first five years, while season tickets increased by a factor of ten. The houses to the right of the photograph were built on land previously occupied by two larger houses called Brightwell and Glebe. Rosedene Avenue, which leads off to the right just before the pillar box, was built partly on Glebe land. (© *Alan Cross*)

London Road, looking east, 6 August 2005. Despite appearances Morden South station still exists between the sorting office and the mosque; if you know where to look, its roof is just visible to the left of the rather straggly fir on the right of the photograph. The road may look relatively unchanged, but it is now a dual carriageway, only one carriageway of which is visible. Considering all the other changes, the houses on the right are remarkably little altered. (*George Hobbs*)

Entrance to Morden Park, London Road, looking south-west, 1949. The bus on route 156 is one of those borrowed from Maidstone Corporation (see page 95). The lodge house in the background guarded the main entrance to Morden Park and the approach to the house. From the lodge a curved sweep led to the eighteenth-century house built by John Ewart. Just to the right of the photographer a footpath led across Morden Park Golf Course, now various playing fields and sports grounds, to Hillcross Avenue. I wonder what the young lad is waiting for. (© *Alan Cross*)

London Road, 11 June 2005. London Road has been straightened and widened for most of its length and seems to have sprouted a lot more clutter in the form of speed cameras, red route notices, etc. The lodge house has gone, but Morden Park House still exists. It is owned by the London Borough of Merton and forms part of Merton College. Not to be confused with Merton College, Oxford (see introduction to Chapter 2), Merton College, Morden Park is a centre for vocational training and is particularly noted for its courses in automotive engineering, specialising in motorcycle excellence. (*George Hobbs*)

Straightening London Road, looking north-east, 1952. The gate to the right of the photograph is the gate just visible above the mound of stones in the upper photograph on page 26. The workman's hut in the centre is parked where the road is being cut through the trees. The white gate in the distance to the left of the photograph was one of the entrances to Morden Park. During the Second World War an anti-aircraft gun was located just inside the grounds. Most ack-ack guns had a calibre of either 3.7 or 4.5in and could fire around eight shells per minute. The location of such guns was an official secret but they made such a din that they were no secret to local residents. (© *Alan Cross*)

London Road, looking north-east, 20 August 2005. The style of housing visible on the right of this photograph was encouraged, providing much needed accommodation between the two world wars. With hindsight the architects were perhaps naive in their stated belief that wide public areas would foster a sense of community and joint 'ownership' far more than individual gardens. It is fascinating that plans for housing in London in 1943 included as 'indispensable' 'a small outside room or store, in which handicrafts could be practised or domestic animals kept'. (*George Hobbs*)

Straightening London Road, looking north-east, 1952. The bends between the George Inn and Chalgrove Avenue were known locally as 'the S-bends'. They were considered to impede the smooth passage of traffic and so were straightened and widened. The cottages in the distance were soon to be demolished by specialist Syd Bishop, and flats built beside the new road. Syd Bishop and Sons Demolition Ltd was established in 1929 and still exists, based at Orpington in Kent. (© Alan Cross)

London Road, 11 June 2005. London Road was straightened and widened at different times to carry the increasing amount of traffic. Despite only one car being visible in the photograph this road is usually very busy. At about the point where the gateposts are visible in the centre of the photograph there used to be a milepost which read '10 Miles to Whitehall'. There is an old house in Cheam called Whitehall and the characters on other mileposts in the area pointing to the Cheam Whitehall match this one, but the distance is only about 4 miles from here. Whitehall in London would usually have been called just 'London' but old maps of the area show another milepost at Stonecot Hill marked as 'Whitehall 11'. Perhaps it's the London Whitehall that is meant after all. (George Hobbs)

Morden Park Cottages, London Road, 17 April 1954. The name is on the cottages but for some reason it's upside down; the signboard is on the wooden fence just to the left of the right-hand garden gate. The chimney pots in the middle and to the right are splendid Victorian copies of a much earlier design. The left set is missing but during the 1920s many such pots were sold as decorative garden ornaments. Maybe the owner of the cottage saw a way of making a quick profit. R.G. Jones was famous locally for providing sound equipment among other things (see introduction to Chapter 4). (© *Alan Cross*)

One of the entrances to Merton College, 11 June 2005. Like many of the buildings bordering the road the cottages were demolished when the road was widened and straightened. Currently, Merton College and its sixth form centre are undergoing a £24 million redevelopment. Work began in February 2005 and is expected to take three years. Designed by Nightingale Associates, who also undertook the renovation work on the Roman Catholic cathedral in Liverpool, the new buildings are to provide classrooms, laboratories and workshops. In this photograph, building work is just visible through the trees. (*George Hobbs*)

Rutland Parade looking towards George Hill, 25 April 1954. Despite claims to be a high-class butcher, Blann's meat was abysmal according to local residents. In local advertisements J. Neil Blann also claimed to be a 'purveyor of English and Colonial meat'. Kangaroo? Perhaps that's what tasted so bad! Blann's is now offices, next to and possibly part of 'Laser Inks'. One of the shops in Rutland Parade was a hairdresser and barber with possibly unique perimeter seating in the men's section: it was made up of seats from the old London buses broken up behind St Lawrence's Church (see page 61). George Hill also had a link with vehicles. It often appeared in the car-chase scenes filmed by Merton Park Studios (see page 106). (© *Alan Cross*)

Corner of Lower Morden Lane and Epsom Road, 25 April 1954. Rutland Parade is in the distance. During the 1980s one of the houses on the right suffered a roof fire serious enough to be featured on the national television news. A few yards to the left of where the photographer is standing is the line of Stane Street, the Roman road which linked London to the coast at Chichester. The line runs through the edge of Morden Park. The park was owned by the Garth family (see page 41) from 1553, although Morden Park House was leased to various occupants from 1780. It was bought by Gilliat Hatfeild in the 1870s before being purchased from the Hatfeild family in 1945 by Merton and Morden Urban District Council. (© Alan Cross)

Corner of Lower Morden Lane and Epsom Road, 11 June 2005. Apart from the ubiquitous road widening very little appears to have changed in the last fifty years. Further north the road is called London Road; the change of name to Epsom Road indicates its importance to race traffic, particularly in the early part of the nineteenth century. Edward VII was very fond of racing and one of the very few people to own winners of both the Derby and the Grand National. The Coronation Cup, run during the Epsom Derby meeting in June, was inaugurated to celebrate Edward VII's coronation. The king would have driven to Epsom Races along this road. (George Hobbs)

Stonecot Hill looking north-east, 5 March 1955. The roadworks are not for road widening – given the small amount of traffic there is no need (yet) – but to build a stopping bay for buses. The junction is an ancient one where a path across the common, now Sutton Common Road, joined the pack route to London. The Woodstock Inn is just out of shot to the right; it may well have been built on the foundations of an earlier hostelry positioned strategically on the corner to serve travellers on the old trackways. (© Alan Cross)

Stonecot Hill looking north-east, 11 June 2005. Stonecot literally means a stone cottage and as Stane Street is thought to run just to the left of the road at this point the names might be connected. The name Stane Street was not Roman, although the road it describes is, but was first used during the twelfth century. Incidentally, the photographer is not standing in the middle of the road. A service road is separated from the main carriageway by a raised island; the photographer is standing on the island. *(George Hobbs)*

Premises of E.S. Fisher & Son, Stonecot Hill, 1958. E.S. Fisher had an extensive timber yard on the north side of what is now Epsom Road, with a high-quality ironmonger's shop almost opposite on the south side. The small shop seen here is situated roughly on the site of the large square sign near the bus in the upper picture on the previous page. The route of Stane Street, the Roman road, passed through the back of Fisher's timber yard. (© Alan Cross)

Premises of Woodstock Motor Company, Stonecot Hill, 20 August 2005. In the mid-1950s Fisher's yard closed and the site was redeveloped as eight luxury maisonettes; one is nearing completion in the upper photograph. The shop and part of the yard were retained and are now a showroom and workshop for second-hand cars. The company also runs its own drag race team called Honeymonster Racing. (George Hobbs)

Stonecot Hill looking north-west, 5 March 1955. Up until the beginning of the twentieth century this was a T-junction, only becoming a crossroads when Tudor Drive was laid out. In about 1949 a steel-framed house was erected at the lower end of Tudor Drive but remained incomplete with the skeletal framework showing in order to demonstrate alternative building methods. It was subsequently dismantled, perhaps as a result of the 1951 government report on non-traditional housing entitled 'The corrosion of steelwork in steel-clad and steel-framed houses'! (© Alan Cross)

Stonecot Hill looking north-west, 11 June 2005. Fifty years ago the junction was quiet enough not to need traffic lights although such traffic control was not unknown. The first traffic lights appeared on 10 December 1868 outside the Houses of Parliament. They looked a little like railway signals with semaphore arms and red and green gas lamps for use at night. In the USA policeman Lester Wire installed the first red-green electric traffic lights in Salt Lake City in 1912, while the first three-colour traffic lights were introduced in New York and Detroit in 1920. The lights were hand operated; automatic traffic lights did not appear for another seven years until installed in Wolverhampton in 1927. In urban areas today you can rarely travel a mile without seeing them. (George Hobbs)

Sports facilities being built, London County Council sports ground, London Road, 25 April 1954. In the *County of London Plan, 1943* the LCC put forward its view that adequate open spaces for rest and recreation were essential for the health of people living in its area and anticipated that interest in sport would increase. It aimed to ensure that town dwellers would be able 'to get from doorstep to open country through an easy flow of open space from garden to park, from park to parkway, from parkway to green wedge and from green wedge to Green Belt'. Morden and its parks were mentioned particularly as forming part of a 'green wedge' which included Nonsuch and Chessington. *(© Alan Cross)*

Vandalised sports facilities, Morden Park, London Road, 11 June 2005. Why do people do this? Only fifty years old and the buildings will almost certainly have to be demolished. Sports facilities are generally good in the area, with Morden Park home to tennis courts, pitches for cricket and football and a swimming pool. Designed by George Lowe & Partners, architects more noted for laying out golf courses and club houses, Morden Park Pool was opened in 1967. Now managed for the council by Greenwich Leisure Ltd, the changing rooms were refurbished in 2005 and a new sports hall planned as part of the complex for 2007. *(George Hobbs)*

The stile in Lower Morden Lane giving onto the footpath to London Road, *c.* 1925. Like many of its modern counterparts the stile is decorative rather than functional now that the gate which undoubtedly flanked it is missing. In the distance two boys and a girl on the footpath stare at the cameraman, but the young man by the tree seems to be more interested in what's happening in the ditch. *(Lilian Grumbridge)*

Entrance to park, Lower Morden Lane, leading to footpath, 6 March 2005. Under the 1949 National Parks and Access to the Countryside Act footpaths were surveyed and recorded onto a definitive map. Before that date only two Justices of the Peace were needed 'to stop up and to sell and dispose of such unnecessary Highway, Bridleway or Footway' (legislation of 1815). Road traffic may have increased but since the late 1940s rights of way must be honoured. As a result this footpath, although now only a short cut across Morden Park, still exists. *(George Hobbs)*

Haywains, Lower Morden Lane, looking towards Cardinal Close, *c.* 1925. Up until the 1930s Morden was still very much a rural community with a relatively low population, most of which worked on the land. An old farm account book of 1850 shows the importance of haying: six men and three women worked for a total of 289 'man' days to gather in the hay. One of the labourers, Richard Furlonger, was then paid 15*s* to thatch the hayrick. Note that the two hay wagons, originally designed to be horsedrawn, are hauled by an early tractor. *(Lilian Grumbridge)*

Footpath from Lower Morden Lane leading to Cardinal Close, 6 March 2005. Eighty years later and only the footpath remains to show any sign that this was once farmland. Rights of way must be honoured even in housing estates, which is why snickets (alleyways) such as this one exist between houses. Interestingly, the law that applies to public rights of way is not the same as that which is applicable to roadside pavements, which are counted as part of the highway. *(George Hobbs)*

Green Lane *c.* 1925. In 1926, 1927 and 1929 the London County Council (LCC) compulsorily purchased an area of 825 acres to build what was to become the St Helier Housing Estate. It was named after Lady Mary St Helier who had been an LCC alderman from 1910 to 1927. The residents of the capital of Jersey thought the name would cause confusion and suggested Jeuneville instead, Lady Mary having been Lady Mary Jeune until her marriage. Youngtown, the literal translation of Jeuneville, might have been quite appropriate. Green Lane was an ancient right of way within the area and over the next ten years or so was transformed into a suburban road. *(Lilian Grumbridge)*

Green Lane, 10 April 2005. Although very different in character, Green Lane is still surprisingly green thanks to the central reservation. The LCC designed the road to leave the option of running trams along the middle, but this was never done. Much of the St Helier estate was designed by G. Topham Forrest, Architect to the Council. He was strongly influenced by Belgian architecture, although his best-known design is probably Chelsea Bridge across the Thames. *(George Hobbs)*

Golf Club House, Merton Park, *c.* 1900. This was the former home of the golf club which ended its days at Morden Park. It was designed by John Sydney Brocklesby, an architect brought in by John Innes to work on Merton Park. Brocklesby won a national competition for a row of cottages he designed and built in Melrose Road. Queen Alexandra came to inspect them and suddenly Brocklesby found himself in demand. He was much influenced by Dutch and Belgian styles of architecture, and the gardens of at least one of his designs were laid out by Gertrude Jekyll. Brocklesby was the first architect approached to design the Church of St John the Divine in Merton, although the plans he produced proved to be too costly to build. The church, rather disgruntled at the unreasonable expense, went elsewhere (see page 62). *(Courtesy Alan Cross)*

Nos 36–50 Maycross Avenue, 11 June 2005. The club house building still exists, now converted into dwellings. When the club house was built the area was largely open fields with few trees. The modern view is not taken from the same angle as the original because the building is now in the centre of an urban housing estate and almost entirely surrounded by mature trees. Brocklesby lived in the area for forty years (see page 106), only moving to Dorset in the first years of the Second World War. He died in 1955. *(George Hobbs)*

Lodge Lane, *c.* 1900. Not only Morden itself but the people and why they visit it have changed a lot in a hundred years. Addressed to Miss J. Greenbury, 3 Nicholas Mount, Hornsea, E. Yorks, this postcard was sent by her young man: 'Dear Miss Greenbury, This is one of the nice walks near where I am staying. Having a champion time. Had a giddy time yesterday seeing the sights in Oxford St. The weather is ripping. Hope you are keeping good. Have you had many clues yet! Yours till death, E.M. Shepherdon.' Clues about what I wonder? *(Courtesy Paul Hughes)*

The Close looking towards Hill Top, 20 August 2005. There were so many lodges in lanes in Morden that it is virtually impossible to be sure now where the upper photograph was taken. But having looked at a range of old maps it is possible that it was a view of what is now The Close. An educated guess, no more. The houses appear to be older than they in fact are and were built in about 1930. Plaques along one of the entrances to the private gardens at the back commemorate previous residents. *(George Hobbs)*

View from the hill, *c.* 1925. The terraced row just visible in the distance is on London Road (see page 18). The photograph was taken from a footpath running roughly north-west from beside the gardens of a house called Hauxley in Central Road across open fields. This is the northern section which leads down to the long footbridge leading over the tracks of the Northern Line depot (see page 85). While Merton early became a suburb of London, Morden's rural character lasted a lot longer, mainly because it was almost entirely owned by the Hatfeild family. *(Courtesy Alan Cross)*

Bury Grove looking towards Bordesley Road, 6 August 2005. The footpath has become a road but the long footbridge is still there and is just visible at the end of the footpath on the left. At first sight the footbridge appears to be surprisingly well used considering that it doesn't lead to the station, but the fact becomes less surprising when you realise that it's the only route to London Road for half a mile in either direction. *(George Hobbs)*

2

Unwillingly to School . . .

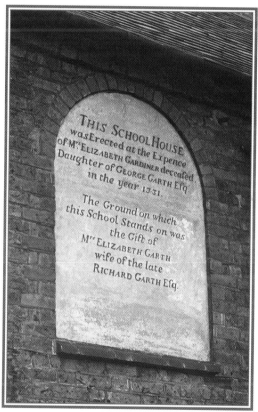

The School House memorial stone, Central Road, 3 February 1968 (see also page 44).
Originally from Wales, the Garth family moved east when Richard Garth became a
Clerk in Chancery. In 1553 he bought the manor of Morden and became Morden's
first resident lord of the manor. In 1718 Elizabeth Gardiner, daughter of
George Garth IV, died and left £300 for the building and endowing of a school; the
first school in Morden to be built for the purpose. The Mrs Garth named on the
memorial stone is niece by marriage to Mrs Gardiner and, on her death in 1776,
herself left £100 to pay the master. (© *Alan Cross*)

The area has long been associated with education. Merton Priory, as well as being a religious establishment, also oversaw the education of the sons of numerous noble houses. Thomas Becket was educated at Merton Priory, as was Nicholas Breakspear who became the only ever English Pope, Adrian IV. One of Merton Priory's alumni, Walter de Merton, became Lord Chancellor of England and Bishop of Rochester. More importantly today, perhaps, is his founding of Merton College, Oxford in 1264. It was only the third of the Oxford colleges to be founded; the two earlier ones are University and Balliol. Merton College's importance is almost as much in its organisation as in its founding. Walter de Merton set up a self-governing community of scholars, with its own statutes and endowment, which lived in buildings laid out in staircases and quadrangles. By doing so he created a model for most of the Oxford and Cambridge colleges founded in the succeeding centuries. Notable members of his college include John Wycliffe, T.S. Eliot, Roger Bannister and J.R.R. Tolkien.

The local Merton College – which is actually in Morden – started life as Merton Technical College and was founded in the early 1970s. Its site was the scene of a particularly selfless act during the war. Pilot Sergeant Peter Walley's plane was hit by enemy action and caught fire. He had time to bail out but knew that, if he did so, the plane would crash onto dense housing with severe loss of life. He therefore chose to stay with the plane and aimed it at Morden Park, the only relatively clear space. He died but probably saved the lives of many civilians. After the college was built a plaque was erected in his honour and unveiled by Group Captain Leonard Cheshire VC. The choice of dignitary was peculiarly appropriate as, apart from his war service, Leonard Cheshire was also a member of Merton College, Oxford.

Merton College, Morden Park provides most of the post-16 education and training in the London Borough of Merton, although courses are open to anyone who can demonstrate an interest in them. Around 7,500 students usually enrol to study for about 12,500 qualifications; in 2005 its youngest student was 14, its oldest 80. Many of the college's courses are vocational and include business, healthcare, catering, engineering and IT. It was rather different 200 years ago when Miss Rutter's boarding school for girls in Morden offered instruction in English, French and needlework.

Famous locally, the Rutlish School for boys owes its existence to two prominent men who could never have met. William Rutlish, embroiderer to Charles II, died in 1687 leaving £400 for 'the putting out poor children borne in this parish apprentice'. Two hundred years later the Rutlish Charity had accumulated far more wealth than there were apprentices to spend it on. John Innes – he of the compost, and a major local employer and benefactor – had taken over the chairmanship of the Rutlish Charity Trustees in 1885 and suggested using the income to found a science school. At first Innes's proposal was opposed, partly because a school was not what Rutlish had originally intended (or he would have founded one himself) and partly because his bequest benefited both sexes whereas the proposed school was to be for boys only. Possibly for that reason, in 1892 the Rutlish Charity opened a cookery school for 'Ladies, Servants and Young Women', which was attended by several school-age girls.

After much wrangling, canvassing of local opinion and discussions with the Charity Commissioners about the legality of the science school plan, the proposals were accepted and Rutlish School was built in Kingston Road. The building was designed by H.G. Quartermain, architect for the John Innes estate, and opened in September 1895. The original building was demolished in the early 1970s, but the school itself moved to the site vacated by the John Innes Horticultural Institute in Watery Lane in 1957. John Innes bequeathed the school sufficient funds to provide an annual scholarship and his house at Manor Farm, purchased by Surrey County Council (before the borough existed), is now part of the school buildings. Rutlish School opened as a science school and continues to specialise in science today; its teaching of mathematics is particularly good and has been recognised in its status as a specialist maths and computing college.

John Innes had other interests connected with education, too. He founded the Boys Club in Kingston Road and paid for instruction in elocution and gymnastics, he provided sports grounds for the use of local schools, and he was manager of the Abbey Road Infants' School. In 1894 the headmistress, Mrs Annie Louise Fleming, wrote in the school logbook: 'Feb 23 . . . The school was visited this morning by J. Innes Esqre who came with the Architect to consult about some details of the plan for proposed improvement to premises.' The architect might once again have been Mr Quartermain.

Various documents about Merton provide tantalising glimpses of other educational establishments. There was, in the middle of the nineteenth century, Morden Hall Academy run by the Revd John White and his son Thomas. Between 1888 and 1896 Miss Godwin ran a School for Ladies in Dorset Road, Merton Park and in 1913 Blakesley House School, Kingston Road was opened by Jack and Alice Dudley. In 1894 the South Wimbledon Institute & Girls' Technical School existed in Norman Road: names are very important and South Wimbledon was thought to sound much better than Merton (see pages 86–7).

The Borough of Merton still makes education a priority. Singlegate Primary School, for example, is new. It was designed by Parsons Brinckerhoff, built by Mansells and finished during the summer of 2002. Its name is much older, however, as it refers to Merton's turnpike: a 'single gate' to distinguish it from the double gates across the road at Wimbledon.

It was during 2002 that the borough's education policy underwent radical revision. For some years the borough operated a policy of First, Middle and Upper Schools. First Schools took pupils aged 4–9, Middle Schools pupils aged 9–13, Upper Schools pupils aged 13–16/18. In 2002 this changed and schools were reorganised into Infant, Junior and Secondary with the corresponding age bands of 4–7, 7–11 and 11–16/18.

The School House, Central Road, 3 February 1968. The school opened in 1731 and probably had twelve pupils to start with, indicating that the parish was both small and rural. One hundred and sixty years later the building had been expanded and the roll had risen to 190 children. By the end of the eighteenth century the little school was not the only educational project for the lower classes in what was still a small village: in 1791 a Sunday school was started by public subscription. (© *Alan Cross*)

The School House, Central Road, 6 August 2005. Remarkably little has changed at the School House if you exclude the growth of the trees. It ceased to be a school in 1910 when Surrey County Council built a new one in London Road. The building on Central Road then became the parish hall. Signs of a portico are just visible above the door to the left and indicate where a porch extended onto the footpath. When London County Council became responsible for the road and footway it would not tolerate encroachment so the porch was removed in about 1930. (*George Hobbs*)

Merton Abbey Primary School, *c.* 1950. The field has only recently been converted back to grass after having been used as allotments during the Second World War. Nowadays low-fat diets are considered healthier but in 1948 Mr Philip Barling OBE persuaded New Zealand farmers and their wives to render and pack into tins dripping which would otherwise have gone to waste. In 1952 the school received eight 40lb tins of fat, a tiny fraction of the 310,000lb of dripping received and distributed. The scheme was started in Dunedin, now more famous as the setting for the film trilogy *Lord of the Rings* (whose author has a connection with Merton – see page 42), and the name and address of the sender were put on each tin so that recipients could write and thank them. *(Courtesy Merton Abbey Primary School)*

The Fort, 9 August 1998. The air-raid shelter visible on the left in the picture above was used as a store room until around 1960. It was then buried underneath 'The Mound' to make the children's play area safer. In 1984 The Mound was transformed into The Fort and twenty years later, in the summer of 2004, the whole area including the air-raid shelter was cleared. The wall to the rear of The Fort borders Merantun Way and was completed during the summer holidays in 1989. *(Courtesy Merton Abbey Primary School)*

Merton Abbey Primary School, *c.* 1980. Note that there is no 'drawbridge' on The Fort and that there are caravans on the site of what is now Staples, the office superstore. Merton Abbey Primary School started life as Abbey Road National Infants School. The school log still exists from 4 August 1891 and lists thirty-nine pupils under the charge of Harriot Markham. Admissions continued throughout August and September of that year until the school was averaging over seventy pupils per week. On 19 April 1872 Annie Louisa Dodd, later to become Mrs Fleming, took over the school on a temporary basis as Mrs Markham was ill. On 1 October the same year she succeeded as headmistress and was to remain in charge for forty-four years. (*Courtesy Merton Abbey Primary School*)

Site of Abbey Road National Infants School, precursor to Merton Abbey Primary School, 10 July 2005. School premises were built on the north corner of Abbey Road and Nelson Grove Road in 1836 and at first consisted of two rooms and a gallery. There were three classes: children over 6 were in the first class, over 5 in the second and over 4 in the third. Once children reached 7 they left the school. By 1873 there were doubts about the suitability of the building. The HMI report, noted in the school logbook for 27 March of that year, states: 'It may be questioned whether the room is warmed sufficiently for Infants in cold weather. Repairs are wanted in the floor.' (*George Hobbs*)

Delivery of temporary classrooms, Merton Abbey Primary School, *c.* 2001. Slices of Portakabins were delivered in convoy along High Path to be bolted together once on site. As the road is both narrow and one way only it was something of a logistical challenge when the lorries queued down the road. The temporary accommodation was needed while the hall was being extended and new classrooms built. Work was completed by August 2002 and the Portakabins removed during the summer. Records at the school mention blithely that it was just after the foundations had gone in that the gas main ruptured. Oh dear! *(Courtesy Merton Abbey Primary School)*

Merton Abbey Primary School, 6 August 2005. On 21 November 1927 Mrs E.A. Waight, Temporary Headteacher, noted in the school's logbook: 'This school opened today at 9 a.m. with the children transferred from the Abbey Road C of E School.' The next few days were much concerned with logistics such as arranging for a fireguard for the 'Babies Room', arranging for keys to the school, school gate and cupboards to be held by the correct people and having the piano tuned. Early the following year consideration was given to 'the asphalting of a pathway leading from the school door to the lavatories' – which were outside. One wall of the toilet block still exists; it is visible to the far left of the photograph. *(George Hobbs)*

Merton Abbey Primary School, 22 November 1977. The school celebrated its golden jubilee in style. The mayor and mayoress visited the school as did Mrs Joan Lovatt who had helped at the opening of the new premises fifty years earlier. After the distinguished visitors had left, the entire school, with the exception of the nursery classes who had their own entertainer, visited Wimbledon Theatre to see *Pinocchio*. Here the mayor, Alderman Peter Kenyon, is talking to Heike Day. *(Courtesy Merton Abbey Primary School)*

Mrs Susan Taylor and the seven-a-side football team, Merton Abbey Primary School, 1979. In their first season in the Merton Schools' Football Association the team came top of the Merton Primary seven-a-side league. The 8- and 9-year-olds look delighted – and no wonder. *(Courtesy Merton Abbey Primary School)*

Tree planting, 30 March 1990. The new wall between Merton Abbey Primary School and Merantun Way looked rather stark (see page 45) so conifers were planted to soften it. Here the Head, Mrs O'Donnell, wields a spade. Each class was responsible for planting a tree, helped by parents, Mrs Harris (Chairman of Governors) and Miss Bareham who was Headteacher at the school for twenty years until 25 July 1989. *(Courtesy Merton Abbey Primary School)*

More spade work. 8 June 1993. William Morris's print works closed in 1939 and the already fragile buildings were further damaged during the war. They were demolished and incorporated into Merton Board Mills, which in turn eventually became the Savacentre site (see page 14). Part of the complex was new housing, built later than the giant hypermarket which is just visible over the fence. Here children from Merton Abbey Primary School bury a time capsule where William Morris's print works once stood. *(Courtesy Merton Abbey Primary School)*

Merton Park Primary School, 1985. Merton Park Primary is very similar in appearance to Merton Abbey Primary, which is perhaps not surprising as both schools transferred to their new buildings in 1927. Merton Park Primary started life as Merton National School and was situated opposite the east end of St Mary's Church in St Mary's Road, now an extension of Church Lane. The school was built in 1870 as the result of a charitable bequest from Richard Thornton, said at his death to be the richest man in England. The National School building no longer exists but its site is remembered in the name of a new cul-de-sac called Old School Close. (*Courtesy Merton Park Primary School*)

Merton Park Primary School, *c.* 1993. The school is in the Merton Park Conservation Area which is a quiet residential neighbourhood with a different character from most of Merton and Morden. Conservation areas were made possible by the Civic Amenities Act, 1967 and Merton Park was designated as such the following year. The Conservation Area is bounded by Kingston Road and Watery Lane to the north and west, and both sides of Dorset Road are included to the east. Merton Park School is on the southern edge. *(Courtesy Merton Park Primary School)*

Merton Park Primary School, 10 July 2005. The school is slightly smaller than the average primary school but has a very good reputation and has received a range of awards for its varied curriculum. The Sport England Activemark Gold rewards the school's efforts to promote the benefits of physical activity, while the Arts Council England's Artsmark recognises the school's commitment to the arts. The school also has a lot of extra-curricular activities – including, as can be seen from the photograph, gardening. *(George Hobbs)*

Morden Farm County Primary School, *c.* 1956. Built in 1938, the school later became Morden Farm Middle School and then, in 2002, amalgamated with Tudor First School to become Aragon Primary School. Exactly what occasioned the dressing up is not now clear; presumably the very young ringmaster with his performing horses is entertaining parents and visitors. Derek Poulter doesn't admit it, but he might just be the back – and front – end of a circus horse. *(Derek Poulter)*

Aragon Primary School, Aragon Road, 11 June 2005. With the current concerns about obesity in children, many schools are trying to encourage pupils to take more exercise during break periods. Consequently far more play equipment is being installed in school playgrounds. Of course bureaucracy has a part to play. Two European Standards, BS EN 1176 and BS EN 1177, specify how the equipment should be made and installed, and what sort of impact-absorbing surface should be used as a surround. It seems that equipment is replacing imagination. *(George Hobbs)*

Opening ceremony, Bishopsford Community School, 22 September 1999. The school was one of twenty-five schools nationwide to be opened under the 'Fresh Start' scheme. The scheme was designed to replace a school closing because of serious weaknesses with one on the same site actively supported by the local education authority, the Office for Standards in Education (Ofsted) and the Department for Education and Skills. In reflective mood is Estelle Morris, Minister for School Standards, and Mrs Siobhan McDonagh, MP for Mitcham and Morden, standing by the plaque Ms Morris has just unveiled. *(Courtesy Bishopsford Community School)*

Pupils entertain MPs, staff and their peers, Bishopsford Community School, 22 September 1999. The school opened in September 1999 after a £10m investment programme. Parents chose from various names suggested for the new school, including Greenfield Community School and Riverbank Community School, before deciding on Bishopsford. Bishopsford Road runs to the east of the school grounds; the school was named after the road and the road after Bishopsford House, the remnants of which are still just about visible at the east end of Poulter Park. *(Courtesy Bishopsford Community School)*

Classroom, Watermeads High School, early 1999. Watermeads School was labelled as a 'failing school' in March 1998 after two Ofsted inspections. Judging by the premises the school was certainly struggling. (*Courtesy Bishopsford Community School*)

Chris Woodhead learning about Greek mythology, 2000. Having held the post of Chief Inspector of Schools since 1994, Mr Woodhead left Ofsted on 30 November 2000 and is now the Sir Stanley Kalms Professor of Education at the University of Buckingham. (*Courtesy Bishopsford Community School*)

Bishopsford Community School, 2000. Judging by the prevalence of English dictionaries this is an English class. The wall at the back of the room displays work on media studies. Although the school is co-educational it does have a higher proportion of girls, which probably explains why no boys are visible in the picture. (*Courtesy Bishopsford Community School*)

Reception, Watermeads High School, early 1999. A harassed receptionist is barricaded in her goldfish bowl. Watermeads closed largely because it failed to meet the minimum standards of 15 per cent A–C grades at GCSE. In 2004 Bishopsford achieved 35 per cent A–C grades and is now one of the top ten consistently improving schools in London. (*Courtesy Bishopsford Community School*)

Reception, Bishopsford Community School, 10 October 2005. Even to a casual visitor, the contrast between Watermeads and Bishopsford could hardly be clearer. Charlene Lish welcomes visitors to the school; the old reception area is behind her to the right. Bishopsford Community School's first Ofsted inspection in February 2003 highlighted good teaching in English, history, music, RE, drama and art. Its extended day programme provides masterclasses for more able students, support for pupils who need extra help, as well as offering the chance for pupils to try something new such as Egyptology or Japanese culture. (*George Hobbs*)

3

Calling the Faithful

St Lawrence's lychgate, *c.* 1950. The noticeboard points out that this is Morden Parish
Church. There has been a church on this site since 1246, although nothing of the
original survives. The entrance to the church and churchyard had a much greater
importance formerly than it does now. In the Middle Ages weddings were conducted
at the church door as a symbolic representation of entering a new life together.
Lychgates were also eminently practical. 'Lych' comes from the old English word for a
corpse; a lychgate was therefore a gate with a roof to shelter a bier or coffin from the
rain. Incidentally, the fences and gates bordering a churchyard are under the control
of the local authority and not the church to which they belong. (© *Alan Cross*)

Merton Priory was obviously the largest religious organisation in the area for many hundreds of years, but had remarkably little direct effect on the faith of local people. It's rather like living next to an international airport – it won't help you get to the shops! For spiritual guidance and help, ordinary people would attend the local parish church. In Merton this would have been St Mary's Church; in Morden, St Lawrence's.

The Church of St Mary the Virgin actually pre-dates Merton Priory, although only by a year or two. Although much altered, it stands where a church has stood for almost 1,000 years. Gilbert, a Norman knight, was granted the manor of Merton in 1114 and rebuilt the church which had fallen into ruin. Perhaps it was the work on his local church that inspired him to found the huge priory of Merton (see introduction to Chapter 1). Many famous people have attended St Mary's, including one not often associated with Merton, the painter Graham Sutherland.

Sutherland senior was a local barrister and the family moved from Streatham, where Graham was born, to Merton Park. Graham Sutherland, who became a Catholic in 1926, was commissioned to produce a number of religious works for churches around the country. In 1962 these culminated in the huge tapestry *Christ the Redeemer Enthroned in Glory* which hangs in Coventry Cathedral. Not everyone likes the tapestry – one visitor called it a 'giant tea towel' – but it is certainly imposing. Sutherland always said that medieval religion influenced his painting, so perhaps some elements of the tapestry were inspired by the ancient church he knew in childhood.

Not all religious buildings in the area are ancient. In fact the largest and most prominent place of worship is less than five years old. The Ahmadiyya Muslim Community has been established in London since 1913. In 1924 the community built Fazl Mosque, known as The London Mosque, which was the first purpose-built mosque in the UK; the few older mosques were converted from earlier buildings. In the last few years of the twentieth century the community chose Morden to be the site of a new mosque complex and the area gained not only a new place of worship but also a popular tourist attraction.

Voted by the *Independent* magazine as one of the world's top fifty buildings, the mosque is a stunning blend of modern and traditional design. It also cleverly reuses part of the buildings that originally occupied the site; one of the minarets, for example, began life as a chimney. Part of the complex of buildings includes rooms used by local organisations, and the mosque manager generously allows businesses use of the car park whenever possible. Funds to pay for the mosque were raised entirely within the community, with children volunteering part of their pocket money and women donating items of jewellery.

A community effort at fund-raising was also a feature of the Methodists' plans for a new church in the area in the early twentieth century. A site was chosen in Martin Way and work began to raise money. The site and building were eventually to cost £4,675 15s 8d and the amounts donated ranged from a single anonymous gift of £1,000 to 3s collected entirely in farthings. With their help the new church was opened on 15 September 1934. A new and larger church was started in 1957 but the original building still exists and is now the church hall.

The 1920s and 1930s were obviously times of spiritual as well as physical growth for Merton and Morden. It was during this period that the Catholic parish of Morden was founded by Fr Brendan Byrne. Afterwards he served for a time in Crayford but returned to the area as parish priest for Sutton in 1955 until his retirement in 1969. The first Catholic church in the area was St Teresa's, Bishopsford Road, which was built in 1931.

In 1880 the Revd C.H. Spurgeon, the famous Baptist evangelist, wrote to the Revd Charles Ingrem: 'near to you at Wimbledon you will find Mitcham and Merton and Morden all needing Gospel Work. As soon as you have got your own little church in working order, start something at each of these places.' Mr Ingrem's first mission at Morden was in 1885 in a disused grocer's shop near the Crown Public House. Mr Gilbert Laws, a solicitor's clerk, later to become the Revd Mr Laws and President of the Baptist Union, canvassed widely for subscriptions to build a Baptist chapel.

Humphrey's Iron Churches of Hyde Park, London were specialists in manufacturing temporary religious buildings for growing areas of population and had some sample buildings on show near Morden. Queen's Road Baptist Church in Wimbledon offered to buy one for Morden Baptists. Rumours have it that the building was 'remaindered' and was therefore discounted in price, but the gesture was still a generous one. In 1896 the 'tin tabernacle' was erected in Crown Road. In 1929 the fellowship moved across the road to School Hall – which still exists – and, only six years later, to the new church opened on 9 March 1935 in Crown Lane. Meanwhile, in 1928 Queen's Road Church, Wimbledon, again generously helped fellow Baptists found a church in Merton Park on the corner of Bushey Road and Botsford Road.

St Lawrence's Church, *c. 1950*. The church is probably fourteenth century, and there is some evidence that originally it had a thatched roof; certainly the tower was once thatched. By the seventeenth century the church had become dilapidated and in 1635 work began to repair it. The original walls were then faced with brick, possibly to replace stone facings which had decayed. The brick walls take none of the weight of the roof which is still supported on the old walls hidden from sight. *(© Alan Cross)*

St Lawrence's Church, 11 June 2005. The extension to the right of the picture, which houses the church centre, was built in 1983. St Lawrence's churchyard contains many interesting gravestones including that of Gilliat Hatfeild (see page 17), Morden's last squire, who died in 1941. Another permanent resident is Captain Alexander Maconochie who in 1840, at his own request, took charge of Norfolk Island, a tiny penal colony midway between Australia and New Zealand. Maconochie had spent some time as a prisoner of war during the Napoleonic Wars and was convinced that prison reform was essential. As a naval captain he had observed that pressed sailors responded to motivation and peer pressure far better than to brutality and fear. He put his ideas into practice on Norfolk Island with startling success and many of his innovations still affect prison conditions today. *(George Hobbs)*

Behind St Lawrence's Church, 1933 or 1934. Unlikely as it sounds, the area behind the church was used for scrapping old London buses; the church tower can just be seen above the middle vehicle. The bus in the centre was a Bean (after the name of the chassis manufacturer), registration number DV 5364. It was acquired second-hand by H.F. Phillips, a small bus operator, in July 1932. On 23 November the same year he received approval to use this bus for route 232 from Dagenham Docks; the roads were of such poor quality that no other operator was interested in running a service over them. When the London Passenger Transport Board (LPTB) was formed in 1933, it mopped up all small operators and the Bean was one of many hundreds of non-standard vehicles acquired. The bus was never run by the LPTB and was quickly disposed of as unsuitable for operation. (© *Alan Cross*)

Behind St Lawrence's Church, 11 June 2005. Nothing remains of the scrapyard and the area is now a haven for wildlife; the church tower is just visible through the trees. Canon T.L. Livermore, who was the first churchman to invite Billy Graham to Britain, became Rector of Morden and St Lawrence's Church in 1949. Canon Livermore remained at St Lawrence's Church for nineteen years, during which time the two daughter churches of St Martin's and Emmanuel were built. (*George Hobbs*)

Foundations, Church of St John the Divine, 1913. Although of poor quality, the photograph is included as it shows an extremely early use of piles made of reinforced concrete. When the church was built the water-table for the area was much higher than it is now and standard foundations would not have supported a building of this weight. Foundation specialists J. & W. Stewart were called in by builders Allen Fairhead & Son to utilise the most up-to-date building methods. So proud was the church of its state-of-the-art foundations that an entire page was devoted to them in a short early guide book. *(Courtesy Church of St John the Divine)*

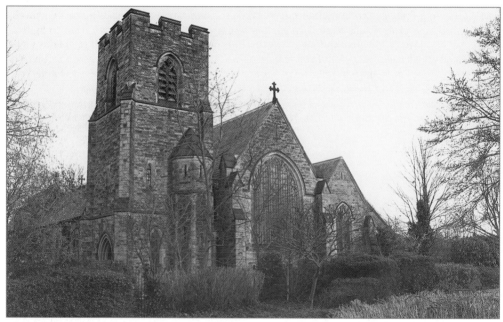

Church of St John the Divine, west end, 24 March 2005. Mr Mackrell had donated the acre of ground for the site in 1905 or 1906 but stipulated that the building should not be started until the monies to complete it were already to hand. He died in 1910 but his wishes were carried out and not until the sum of £10,000 was raised did construction start. The building was to have been finished by May 1914 but a builder's strike delayed matters and the opening service was conducted by the Bishop of Southwark on 31 October 1914. Incidentally, it was Mr Mackrell's wish that the church should be dedicated to St John the Divine. *(George Hobbs)*

Church of St John the Divine, interior, October 1914. The church was designed to seat about 500 people, with fixtures and fittings all designed by the architect. Harry Hems & Sons of Exeter made the font, pulpit, lectern and altar and delivered them in time for the opening of the church, but the choir and clergy stalls were delayed as seventeen of the firm's workmen went to fight in the First World War. The pulpit and font were given in memory of John Mackrell by relatives and friends, while the lectern was a gift from Rutlish School (see introduction to Chapter 2). The solid oak retable above and behind the altar was presented to the church by Captain Hyde Parker and is supposed to come from Nelson's ship *Victory*. *(Courtesy Church of St John the Divine)*

The Revd R.H.M. Langley, *c.* 1930. At first, the Church of St John the Divine was a daughter church of St Mary's. Mr Langley was the church's first vicar, taking up his office in 1925 and remaining for sixteen years. The parish was expected to grow much more than it actually did as the area between High Path and Morden Hall Park became an industrial estate rather than the expected housing. On 22 July 1941 Mr Langley was appointed vicar of Christ Church, Annscroft, near Shrewsbury. He was succeeded by the Revd G.A. Westrup who was inducted on 28 September 1941. *(Courtesy Church of St John the Divine)*

Church of St John the Divine, interior, possibly 1992. Apart from the disappearance of the hatchments and pews little appears to have changed in eighty years, but the detailed differences are quite extensive. Look at the east window, the ceiling, the chancel arch and the nave columns. The beam from *Victory* (see page 63) is still within the church but has been moved to near the font. The Revd Langley was particularly interested in education so he would be pleased that the pupils of Merton Abbey Primary School regularly visit the church. *(Courtesy Merton Abbey Primary School)*

The Vicarage, Church of St John the Divine, *c.* 1950. The Revd Langley supervised the building of his vicarage although there appear to be no records of where he actually stayed to do so. The land for the vicarage was also donated by John Mackrell. At the front of the church a delightful, quiet garden with shrubs and a winding path has fairly recently been laid out. The inscription reads: 'officially opened by Rt Revd Peter Price Bishop of Kingston accompanied by Cllr Sheila Knight, Mayor of Merton, and Mr Roger Casale MP, 9 May 1998.' Set into the path are images of shoals of fish – a rebus on Mr Mackrell's name? (© *Alan Cross*)

Site of old vicarage, 6 August 2005. While this book was being put together the old vicarage of St John the Divine was demolished. Described as a cork in a bottle it stood in the way of valuable building land so, after several years of wrangling, permission was granted to knock it down. It's a pity because it was a lovely building. The new vicarage is on the left out of the way of the through route to what planners hope will be new housing. The roof of Merton Abbey Primary School is just visible over the hedge to the right. (*George Hobbs*)

Site of Emmanuel Church, looking north, 1949 or 1950. Dudley Drive is in the background. The first church was a modest building designed to provide the residents around Stonecot Hill with somewhere to worship until a larger church could be built. It would then become the church hall. For more than ten years the congregations worshipped in the little building while they raised money, firstly to pay off the original loan and then to pay for a new church. Canon Alan Mellows was Emmanuel's minister from 1950 to 1954. (© Alan Cross)

Emmanuel Church Hall, 11 June 2005. Relegated to its intended use as a church hall, the building has changed remarkably little over fifty years. Stonecot Hill is now a bustling residential community but at the beginning of the last century it was far more rural. Stonecot House was reputed to be haunted and stood near the top of Stonecot Hill about where Stonecot Close is now. Mrs White lived there in 1910 and was held in awe by her few neighbours because she had a black butler. (George Hobbs)

Stone-laying ceremony, Emmanuel Church, 14 April 1962. The stone is on the north side of the church facing the footpath. The simple inscription reads: 'This stone was laid by the Churchwardens of Morden H.M. Collins and R.F. Moss 14th April 1962.' At this time Emmanuel was a daughter church of St Lawrence's and so 'churchwardens of Morden' meant churchwardens at St Lawrence's. Six years earlier, on 19 May 1956, Mr Collins, accompanied by fellow churchwarden Mr J.H. Curnow, laid a similar stone at the building of St Martin's Church in Camborne Road. *(Courtesy Emmanuel Church)*

Building Emmanuel Church, 1962. In the parish magazine for September 1956 the outstanding loan for building the hall was noted as having been reduced to £1,400. The writer went on to say: 'we are thus within sight of clearing the loan well before the end of 1957, and before long plans must certainly be considered for the new church itself.' Six years later and the church is being built. This view looks south-east to St Cecilia's Catholic Church on the other side of the road. *(Courtesy Emmanuel Church)*

Building Emmanuel Church, 1962. The area the church was being built to serve was the Morden Park Estate, built by G.T. Crouch Ltd. in the late 1930s. It was called the Tudor estate, which explains many of the road names in the area. In its sales brochure, Crouch excelled in hyperbole: 'Morden Park Estate is supreme amongst modern Housing Estates because it embodies the experience, judgement and vast resources of one of the greatest of building firms, Messrs. G.T. Crouch.' Luxury was simpler then. Kitchens had 'the famous Crouch kitchen cabinet', a gas copper and coal box. Included with the 'lovely bathroom' was a soap holder and toothbrush rack. *(Courtesy Emmanuel Church)*

Emmanuel Church, 10 July 2005. The architect was K.C. White, now the K.C. White Partnership. The firm has been responsible for the design of other churches in the area, most recently St Paul's in Roundshaw Park, Wallington, which was opened in January 2003 by the Rt Revd Tom Butler, Bishop of Southwark. Emmanuel Church was also opened by the then Bishop of Southwark, the Rt Revd Mervyn Stockwood, on 8 December 1962. The photograph is taken from a slightly different angle from that above as trees have grown so as to obscure the building from the same angle. *(George Hobbs)*

Wedding of Malcolm Thomas and Jeanette Bailey, Emmanuel Church, 18 April 1987. The following year the couple's first child Matthew was christened at Emmanuel. Standing near the altar is the Revd Ray de Vial, minister 1984–94. It was his first parish as he was what the Church unflatteringly terms a 'geriatric', i.e. someone ordained later in life. He had previously worked for some years as an engineer. The banners around the wall had been made during 1983 and 1984, following a suggestion by the previous minister the Revd Howard Norton that the bare plaster needed cheering up. Sixteen were made, with eight being displayed at one time. The first was hung on Good Friday 1983. *(Courtesy Emmanuel Church)*

Emmanuel Sunday School, 1982. Pictured here are, among others: 1 Karen Searle, 2 Paul Grear, 3 Simon Pickitt, 4 Rachel Grear, 5 Christine (or possibly Justine) Coles, 6 Alison Weller, 7 Tony Budden, 8 Christine Walsh (now Christine Nicholas). Morden Sunday schools were founded in 1791 by the Revd Dr John Witherington-Peers MA who was Rector of Morden 1778–1835 and died in 1837. Sunday schools had been around since the fifteenth and sixteenth centuries but it was Robert Raikes who used his position as proprietor and editor of the *Gloucester Journal* to publicise their work. After his first editorial in 1783 Sunday schools were established incredibly quickly and the London Society for the Establishment of Sunday Schools was founded in 1785 to co-ordinate and develop the work. Emmanuel Church still has a thriving Sunday school today. *(Courtesy Emmanuel Church)*

Parish Hall, formerly the Mission Church, Pincott Road, *c.* 1914. In 1884 John Mackrell (see page 62) helped build the Mission Church in Nelson's Fields. The area encompassed the grounds of Merton Place, Nelson's former residence (see introduction to Chapter 1) and was named Nelson's Fields accordingly. The notice above the porch reads 'St Mary's Mission Hall' as at that time the whole of Merton was served by St Mary's Church. When the Church of St John the Divine was built, the Mission Hall became St John's parish hall until replaced by the current parish hall in High Path. *(Courtesy Church of St John the Divine)*

Site of Parish Hall, Pincott Road, 10 July 2005. Before redevelopment Nelson's Fields contained what would politely be called high-density housing and, less politely, slums. Roads were narrow and filthy, terraced housing was cramped, and dwellings were insanitary. Rebuilding of the area began in 1953, but the original housing in Pincott Road still existed into the sixties. By 1965 the buildings had been demolished and replaced by the High Path estate. *(George Hobbs)*

Express Dairy, London Road, 16 June 1954. The Express Country Milk Supply Co. was established in London in 1864 by George Barham. It became Express Dairy Company Ltd in 1892. From 27 March 1954 Express Dairy had a three-track siding onto which trains could be diverted from Morden South station. Milk arrived in tankers by rail and was bottled before being distributed for local delivery. Empty tankers had to continue to St Helier station before using the crossovers south of the station to return. (© Alan Cross)

Baitul Futuh Mosque, London Road, 11 June 2005. Baitul Futuh is one of the largest mosques in Europe and can accommodate up to 10,000 people. The late head of the worldwide Ahmadiyya community, Hadhrat Mirza Tahir Ahmad, laid the foundation stone on 19 October 1999, while the current head, Hadhrat Mirza Masroor Ahmad, inaugurated the mosque in October 2003. The Muslim community has tried to consider local residents while still practising their religion as, for example, in the call to prayer. It is still performed, but inside the mosque rather than from one of the minarets so that locals are not disturbed. *(George Hobbs)*

Farm, known as The Kennels, Lower Morden Lane, *c.* 1925. The keeping of pigs has been a feature of the area since the Middle Ages when the area was heavily wooded and hogs were turned out to feed in the undergrowth (see introduction to Chapter 1). There has been speculation that the house was the surviving end of a much larger building which originally would have extended further to the left; it certainly looks like it. The building was vacated on 2 January 1934 after being gutted by fire. *(Lilian Grumbridge)*

Morden Park Baptist Church, Lower Morden Lane, 5 March 2005. Founded in November 1959, Morden Park Baptist Church has a congregation of about a hundred. The Baptist Church first came about when John Smyth, who had been a scholar at Cambridge University, became dissatisfied with the Established Church and fled to Amsterdam to escape persecution. He died abroad but his friend and fellow believer Thomas Helwys returned to London and founded the first Baptist church in Spitalfields in 1612. There are now about 160,000 Baptists in the UK. *(George Hobbs)*

4

A Transport of Delight

Oops! London Road, *c.* 1950. Judging by the damage, something ran into the side of this Ford
Anglia with some force. The first Anglia made after the Second World War, the E04A, was
cheaply priced and consequently very popular. Its sidevalve 993cc engine was said to
be capable of speeds of a mile a minute; 60mph might not be considered much today but it
wasn't bad half a century ago. The earliest officially recorded motoring fatality happened not
far away on 17 August 1896, when Mrs Bridget Driscoll of Old Town Croydon was run over
and killed by a Roger-Benz car at Crystal Palace. (© *Alan Cross*)

'Those who visited this part . . . found roads marked out but not made up, field paths traversing which they had to climb over gates and stiles which guarded railway lines, along which half-a-dozen trains meandered daily . . .' So said the Revd Charles Ingrem when he visited the area in 1885.

From the transport point of view the area was not always as sleepy as this word-picture indicates. By 1800 the Wandle valley was heavily industrialised with about forty factories or mills producing textiles, metals, snuff, etc. Efficient means of transporting these goods were desperately needed. The only roads were cart tracks which meant that the preferred means of moving goods was by water. The River Wandle is wide and flows swiftly but is also shallow and so not navigable by barges. The factory owners therefore first proposed digging a canal.

One of the leading canal engineers at the time was William Jessop who was approached to produce a feasibility study. Digging the canal was not a problem, although the porous nature of the soil would require that the canal be carefully lined. Ironically in view of the nearness of the river, the main problem was finding an adequate supply of water. Jessop's report says: 'Strong objections would arise to taking water from the streams that feed the River Wandle, the works on which are perhaps more valuable than any others within an equal compass in the kingdom.' He might be flattering his employers but he had a point; remove water from the river and you reduce the motive power of the mills and thus their efficiency and rate of production. Jessop suggested using a railway instead: 'Railways . . . have many years been in use . . . but lately they have been brought to the degree of perfection, which now recommends them as substitutes for canals; and in many cases they are much more eligible and useful.'

Railways at the time meant horse-drawn wagons running on iron rails. Today, railway rolling stock has flanged wheels to prevent it leaving the track. Early railways needed carts which were able to run on road as well as rail and so could not amend the wheels of their vehicles. The rails themselves were therefore built with a raised flange on their inside edge to stop the wheels of the carts falling off the trackway. Railways, usually with wooden rails, had been around since 1603 but had always been privately owned and built to serve a mine or quarry, etc. Jessop's proposal was the first time a railway had been suggested as a commercial venture where anyone could use it on payment of a toll. He stated that 'one horse on an iron railway will draw as much at an average as 8 horses on a common Turnpike Road'.

The Surrey Iron Railway opened on 26 July 1803 and ran for 8½ miles. Tolls ranged from 1d per ton per mile for dung, to 3d per chaldron per mile for coal. A chaldron is equivalent to 36 bushels (each bushel is 8 gallons); the modern British equivalent is 1.309 cubic metres. Apart from the opening ceremony when the owners travelled along the line in wagons, the railway did not carry passengers. It closed in 1839 when competition from more efficient steam railways made it uneconomical.

Railways have played a huge part in the development of the area, particularly in Merton. Two different railway companies opened lines. The London & South Western Railway started at Waterloo and ran through Wimbledon to the South West, while the London Brighton and South Coast Railway had a branch line joining Wimbledon and Croydon. Unusually, the section along what is now Merantun Way was owned jointly by the two companies. The helix car park next to The Tower (see page 14) at the east end of Merton High Street is still called the 'coal yard car park'. It was built on the old coal yard on the loop line which closed. The line went from Tooting to Merton Park on the Tooting to Wimbledon line.

Until the building of the Channel Tunnel, Morden stood at the southern end of the longest continuous railway tunnel in the world. The Northern Line stretches for 17¼ miles but might not have been the area's only underground line if plans for the extension of the District Line had gone ahead. In 1910 an Act of Parliament was passed granting permission for the construction of a 5½ mile railway line between Wimbledon and Sutton through Merton and Morden. Minor work was started at Wimbledon in 1913 and, by 1914, the land was purchased and fenced. The route was planned to take in the current South Merton and Morden South stations, although they were to be called Merton Park and Morden respectively. A station to be called Elm Farm was also planned for Love Lane, slightly south of the current St Helier station.

When the railway was proposed most of the route was still open country and the report said that this part of the line required 'speculative building on a considerable scale before it can afford any satisfactory amount of traffic to the railway'. Plans were drawn up and carefully costed and the line would almost certainly have gone ahead if the First World War had not intervened. The route was eventually taken over by the Southern Railway.

Morden is further away from train and tram than its northern neighbour and so relies more extensively on buses for its public transport. London Transport Green Line Coaches were available for longer distances; they stopped less frequently to improve the journey time and had a minimum fare to discourage passengers only wanting to travel locally. Before the Second World War route 726 went from Baker Street through Morden to Dorking. During the war the coaches had a far more unusual connection with the area. R.G. Jones provided sound equipment locally (see page 27) but during 1943 was contracted to refit Green Line coaches. They were then loaned to the American Red Cross who painted them grey and renamed them 'Clubmobiles'. Each vehicle was fitted with a microphone, loudspeakers, a wireless and gramophone, electric cooker and electric donut-making machine. R.G. Jones certainly fitted the sound equipment and may also have done the rest of the work.

The Clubmobiles were used to service US personnel in the UK and each day would visit various camps and serve hot coffee, donuts, cigarettes, candies, playing cards and US newspapers. They were staffed by a driver and two girls; the driver was accommodated at the various camps visited but the girls had sleeping accommodation in two bunks fitted into the coaches. There were fifty-five Clubmobiles in total. R.G. Jones probably shared the refitting with another firm as each coach took about a week to do.

Locals can choose to ride on buses, trains, trams or use their cars, but the area's relationships with its transport have not always been happy ones. A gravestone in St Lawrence's Church commemorates a Frenchman, Augustin Pascal le Page, who was killed crossing the railway line on 26 June 1966.

Merton Abbey station, 23 August 1927. The station was reputed to have been built on the site of the Chapter House of Merton Priory – despite the name it was never an abbey. The station opened on 1 October 1838 as part of the Tooting, Merton and Wimbledon Railway. In spite of appearances the LSWR 0–4–4T, number E251, M7 class locomotive is about to *push* its two coaches west to Wimbledon. 'Push-pull' trains were occasionally used on short lines to save having to run the engine round at each end. When the locomotive is pushing, the driver is not in the cab but in the specially adapted end coach – the 'front' of the train – and controls the throttle and brake on the engine by remote control. *(Courtesy Merton Abbey Primary School)*

Merantun Way, 10 July 2005. Looking west this is roughly the site of Merton Abbey station. It's relatively unusual for a railway line to get a new lease of life as a road – more are reused as footpaths and cycle paths, which this cyclist would probably prefer – but this is a useful arterial route. One of the most pleasant cycle paths in the area is the Wandle Trail running alongside the River Wandle. On the path behind Octavia Road is a blue roundel sunk into the ground, which says: 'The Wandle Trail "Sutton Cycling Club Starts group Age 6-12 Cycle up to 10 miles some Saturdays And particularly enjoy the bridges"' [*sic*]. *(George Hobbs)*

Merton Abbey station, 23 August 1927. Few passengers used this line after Collier's Wood underground station was opened on the Northern Line on 13 September 1926. The station was closed on 3 March 1929, although the line remained open for freight traffic until 1975. In 1908 the stationmaster here was Mr G.K. Dewdney; he and his family lived in the station building, just visible over the top of the coaches. After the station was closed the house continued as a dwelling for a time and was also used as a goods office. *(Courtesy Merton Abbey Primary School)*

Merton Park tram stop, 19 June 2005. Despite appearances, the building in the background on the left is not the same one as appears behind the train in the top photograph. All the station houses on the line were built as clones of each other; this one was at Merton Park station and is now a very nice residence. The line depicted in the top photograph traced a course between the two buildings in the lower photograph (although the row of houses on the right has been built within the last four years) and joined the Croydon to Wimbledon line behind the photographer. This latter is now part of Tramlink. Tram number 2538 has come from Wimbledon and is heading away from the photographer towards Elmer's End via Croydon. *(George Hobbs)*

Merton Park station building (see previous page), 10 July 2005. From being vandalised and covered with graffiti, the building has been sympathetically restored and retains many original features including the canopy. The course of the line shown in the large photograph ran to the left of this building but access is restricted as it is now private ground. Modern terraced housing of a similar style to that in the centre of this photograph now occupies the track bed. The station served a well-populated area and was particularly busy during the rush hour; in 1969, for example, its staff issued 151,000 tickets. *(George Hobbs)*

Merton Park station, 2 March 1929. Merton Park station started life as a junction, with one line looping back to Tooting. The Tooting branch closed to passenger traffic on 2 March 1929; the class M7 locomotive no. 243 in the photograph is working one of the last trains. Opened on 1 October 1868, the station was first called Lower Merton. John Innes, businessman, philanthropist and unofficial squire, owned a lot of property in the area and thought the name sounded too down-market. On his persuasion it was changed to Merton Park on 1 September 1887. (© *H.C. Casserley*)

Dundonald Road level crossing, 21 June 1924. The class 415 LSWR 4–4–2T locomotive no. 058 has left Wimbledon station and is pushing its carriages towards Merton Park; the red rear lamp is visible just above the left buffer. In railway parlance this is a 14-chain curve. A chain is equivalent to 22 yards so this meant that the radius of the curve was 14 × 22 or 308 yards. The measurement is called a chain because that's precisely what it was; surveyors carried 'land chains' made of long rigid sections joined by short flexible links. Rope stretches and wood expands and warps but a chain measurement taken properly is always exact. *(© H.C. Casserley)*

Dundonald Road level crossing, 10 July 2005. Tram number 2547 is leaving Dundonald Road tram stop en route to Elmer's End. The trams are numbered in sequence from 2530, which follows on directly from the numbering used on the London trams which ceased operation on 5 July 1952. Dundonald Road was formed out of what was originally Lower Worple Road; a 'worple' is a field path, but why the road was renamed is something of a mystery. *(George Hobbs)*

Opening of Merton relief road, February 1989. Called Merantun Way (see page 78), the road ran on the track bed of the old railway line and was opened by Transport Minister Peter Bottomley. Angela Rumbold MP, the Mayor Councillor Allan Jones and David Sainsbury were also present. The photograph is a snapshot, probably taken from the grounds of Merton Abbey Primary School, and not helped by being straight into the sun, but the car on the right is possibly a Humber. *(Courtesy Merton Abbey Primary School)*

Merantun Way, 19 June 2005. Savacentre and the relief road were constructed at the same time; Merantun Way was an access route for customers to the shopping centre being built at its north-east end. Savacentre contributed £6.5m towards the cost of building the road which took thirteen months to complete. Both road and shopping centre opened in February 1989 (see page 15). The original intention had been to continue the new road west beyond Morden Road to join Kingston Road somewhere near the junction with Dorset Road but this was never done. *(George Hobbs)*

Corner of London Road and Central Road, *c.* 1950 (see also title page). Horse-drawn delivery vehicles were still relatively common after the Second World War, but were rapidly replaced by horsepower of a different kind. This horse-drawn vehicle is certainly designed to carry goods rather than passengers and might be a dray. It is tempting to assume that these are shire horses from Young's brewery whose stabling is behind the Ram Brewery in Wandsworth, a few miles to the north. It's unlikely, however, as, apart from the distance, Young's shires are almost invariably black or black and white. *(Derek Poulter)*

Corner of London Road and Central Road, 19 June 2005. Not a very interesting photograph, is it? This sort of road widening is typical of much of Merton and Morden. The old house in the background of the photograph above has long since been demolished to widen the road. Although this is a busy junction the photographer waited almost an hour in the hope that an interesting vehicle would pass. None did, although a Morris Minor estate Traveller is turning right into Central Road. In the foreground to the right is Miss Reckitt's memorial horse trough in its new position; it is shown in its original position on the title page. *(George Hobbs)*

Carriage sheds, Northern Line depot, 16 May 1948. In 1938 the Northern Line was modernised with new rolling stock, known (appropriately) as the '1938 stock', which can just be seen inside the sheds. They were the first to have control equipment under the floor to free space for more seats. More cars of this type were manufactured than almost any other design of train in the world and, at the time of writing, 1938 stock tube trains are still in use on the Isle of Wight. The two carriages in the foreground were of the type replaced by the 1938 stock and by 1948 were being used for maintenance duties. During the Second World War they saw service as a sort of mobile café: they were converted to carry refreshments to those who used the tube tunnels as air-raid shelters. *(© Alan Cross)*

Carriage sheds, Northern Line depot, 19 June 2005. The tube train visible on road 18 was built in 1995. The most obvious difference to earlier stock is that the doors are hung outside the body of the train rather than opening within a pocket inside it. The arrangement means that the working mechanism is open to the elements, but does make maintenance easier as well as providing passengers with an additional 2in of room on either side of the carriage. Two inches may not sound much but any extra space makes a difference to squashed commuters. *(George Hobbs)*

E/1 car 1814, Merton High Street turning out of Merton Road, 9 December 1950. The post office in the background is situated within the building that houses South Wimbledon underground station. The line is double track at this point but narrows to single track behind the photographer. The box visible halfway up the pole on the left is a kind of traffic light for the tram driver or motorman. Two horizontal lights indicate that the single-track section is occupied; two diagonal lights that the track is clear and thus safe for the motorman to proceed. (© *Alan Cross*)

Corner of Merton High Street and Merton Road, 19 June 2005. The post office is now an off-licence but the underground station still exists. Merton seems to be very ephemeral as South Wimbledon station is at one end of Merton High Street, while Collier's Wood station is at the other. To redress the balance some Merton residents refer to Wimbledon as 'North Merton'. The Horse and Groom was known as the Bricklayers' Arms until 1882 and is now the Kilkenny Tavern. It is popular with actors, particularly those from *The Bill* which is filmed locally (see page 105). *(George Hobbs)*

E/1 car 1841, Merton Road, 9 December 1950. The single-track section clearly visible in this photograph was unusual in London and lasted for about 200 yards. Also clearly visible to the left of the photograph is a traction pole doing double duty as a traffic light for non-rail traffic coming down Merton Road. Hanging on this side of the traction pole is a bamboo pole. Wood does not conduct electricity so such poles were hung at intervals around the tramway system in case crews ever needed to manipulate the trolley or even the overhead wiring. (© *Alan Cross*)

Merton Road, 19 June 2005. Fewer bicycles and fewer pedestrians than fifty years ago, but not that many more cars. Incidentally, Terpsichore House, 240 Merton Road, was the headquarters of the British Dance Council, the governing body for the UK's dance teachers, although at the time of writing the building is unoccupied. Unsurprisingly, Terpsichore was the muse of dance and song. (*George Hobbs*)

Morden station, 1931–2. Charles Holden, who in 1931 went on to design buildings for the University of London, was the architect given the task of developing a distinctive 'look' for station buildings which could be used flat, as at Morden, or on a corner as at South Wimbledon (see page 86). Holden came up with what was known as the folding screen design. Portland stone was selected for the façade because it weathered well, was at least partly cleaned by the action of rain and looked good when floodlit at night. Morden station was opened in June 1927 by Lieutenant-Colonel J.T.C. Moore-Brabazon MP, parliamentary secretary to the Minister of Transport. *(Courtesy Paul Hughes)*

Morden station, 22 May 2005. The building was designed and built to be able to support additional storeys and these were added in the early 1960s. From the beginning Morden station was intended as a transport interchange with through road/tube tickets, although the London Passenger Transport Board (LPTB) was not entirely happy with the way it was working. In a letter to Charles Holden in May 1940 Frank Pick, Vice-Chairman and Chief Executive of the LPTB said: 'We have not yet solved for example interchange in comfort and convenience between road and rail vehicles – Morden [is] deficient in this sense.' Mr Pick would be upset to learn that nearly seventy years later, it still is. In spite of the complete absence of buses, Morden station is still a busy bus terminal and interchange – but not on Sundays! *(George Hobbs)*

London General Omnibus Company (LGOC) bus number B2609, Woodstock Inn *c.* 1920. Before the underground station was developed Morden was mainly fields with few bus services. The number 107 above the driver's head indicates the route number; at first route 107 operated only on Sundays from Clapham Common to Dorking. At an optimistic average speed of 10mph the journey would have taken a couple of hours or so. Volume of traffic means that the journey time by road would be very much the same today, although the journey itself would be rather less pleasant. This is the 107A which ran daily from May 1915. (© *Alan Cross*)

Bedford OB, Duple, Dorking, 1 May 2000. Day trips to Dorking via Morden in old buses are still popular. KYE 905 was bought by a Tottenham-based company in 1950 but is now privately owned. Nostalgiabus are based in Mitcham and used to operate a Sunday service which combined transport to Dorking with a sightseeing tour of the Surrey hills, ending at Guildford. The name of one of the shops in the background is particularly appropriate. (*George Hobbs*)

AEC Regal coach, The Woodstock, 8 March 1948. The coach has been hired by London Transport from Carshalton & Wallington Coaches Ltd. to operate a short working of route 93 between The Woodstock and Wimbledon War Memorial. After the Second World War London Transport's bus fleet was rather more than life-expired. Between 1947 and 1949, as a stopgap while new deliveries caught up, several hundred touring coaches were hired from private coach operators. During the week the coaches were used as temporary buses and at weekends were released back to their owners for private hire. Bus passengers benefited by the arrangements. The comfortable seating and luxurious appointments were of a far higher standard than the utility buses they'd been used to. (© *Alan Cross*)

The Woodstock, 20 August 2005. The Woodstock and its car park have changed very little over the years so the photographer has included the plaque on the wall to the far right of the picture. The inscription is rather flowery but concludes: 'This tablet was erected by order of the Borough Council on the occasion of the 21st anniversary of the granting of the charter. Alderman D. Sparks M.B.E., J.P. Mayor.' The plaque was erected in 1934 and marks the approximate boundary of the Borough of Merton with that of Sutton and Cheam. (*George Hobbs*)

London General Omnibus Company (LGOC) bus number S179, Morden station, May 1930. With solid tyres, wooden seats on the upper deck and poor roads, passengers might have expected to be jolted unbearably, but the S-types apparently gave quite a smooth ride. The driver using the starting handle is wearing a white hat which, together with an optional white coat, was standard in the summer. (© *Alan Cross, from the W. Noel Jackson collection*)

'Lowbridge' Daimler, London Transport fleet number D130, Morden station, 2 February 1952. Route 127 ran under the rail bridge at Worcester Park station which was too low for standard double-deckers. As a result London Transport bought some Lowbridge Daimlers. Not only were such buses 1ft 1in lower than the standard height of 14ft 6in but the sloping radiator made them longer than the regulation 26ft maximum length by just under 1in. As a result special permits had to be issued by the police for each route on which Daimlers operated within the London area. For the Lowbridge Daimlers it was not an onerous task, however; London Transport only had ten, all dedicated to route 127. (© *Alan Cross*)

Morden station forecourt, 19 June 2005. Built by East Lancashire Coach Builders in 2001, EVL 4 'curtseys' at the kerb – when it can get to the kerb – so that anyone with mobility difficulties can board. Because the floor is very low the wheels intrude into the passenger space very noticeably. The bus is wider, longer and heavier than its double-decked predecessors, but actually seats fewer passengers. *(George Hobbs)*

RT 4655, London Road, 9 January 1954. Licensed on 4 January 1954, this bus had only been in service for five days when the photograph was taken. The first RT, RT1, came into service on 9 August 1939 and 4,825 were eventually built. RTs were gradually replaced during the 1960s and 1970s, the last few being withdrawn in April 1979. The first RTs had a roof route-number box (see page 97), but later ones used the display configuration shown here. And why 'RT'? No one really knows, but one wag, tongue-in-cheek, said that it stood for Reliable Transport after the hotchpotch of the war years. *(© Alan Cross)*

EVL 52, London Road, 19 June 2005. Everything changes and yet everything stays the same; compare this view with the bottom picture on the previous page. Buses on route 93 still stop here en route to Priory Road, North Cheam, but the bus is new, the shelter is new, the road has been widened and the building on the other side of the road has been refurbished or rebuilt. There have been changes even since this photograph was taken; the Safeway store on the left is now Sainsbury's. The only inanimate object from the era of the previous photograph is the photographer's 1950s bike leaning against the bus shelter. *(George Hobbs)*

Rosehill Co-op, 19 June 2005. Buses still pass the Morden Co-op as in the photograph at the foot of the previous page, but now do so at Rosehill. Stemming originally from a group of Rochdale weavers, the Co-operative Group has expanded into a range of activities from haberdashery to houses and from finance to funerals. The Co-op is even teaming up with ScottishPower to build a windfarm at Coldham in Cambridgeshire. *(George Hobbs)*

Two utility Daimlers (left) and one new one, Morden station forecourt, 22 July 1949. The new Daimler on the right was one of three purchased by Maidstone Corporation, but London Transport was so short of buses that Maidstone had to wait! All three already sported Maidstone livery, so among hundreds of red double-deckers were three painted mustard and cream. On the left in the background is the public garage which was built to serve Morden station. Owned by Underground subsidiary Morden Station Garage Ltd, it opened on 31 July 1927 and was intended to provide parking for commuters to encourage them to use the tube. It had spaces for more than 300 cars plus 200 motorbikes and bicycles. Almost from day one it was oversubscribed. (© *Alan Cross*)

Morden station forecourt, 19 June 2005. Morden station is still a very busy bus interchange and sees a variety of different buses. The site of the public garage is now a shopping precinct, traffic and street furniture have both proliferated and, from the way the roads are fenced, walking appears to be actively discouraged. (*George Hobbs*)

Kenley Road, April 1949. LT132 open staircase bus from 1930 waits to take passengers to Epsom Downs. LT stood for 'long type' meaning that the bus was longer than average and so had three axles rather than the more usual two. After the Second World War the special raceday service had so many passengers that there wasn't room for them to wait in the station forecourt. Racegoers were directed to walk around the back of the station and along the footpath to Kenley Road where buses were waiting for them. To the right of the photographer, railings were erected to ensure that the queues of racegoers remained orderly. In the 1940s the fare to Epsom Downs was 1s each way. (© *Alan Cross*)

Kenley Road, 19 June 2005. Kenley Road and the surrounding area was originally laid out by John Innes who planted the chestnuts which still line the road. The fenced-off area is the station car park and the road to the right leads to modern housing. Morden Hall Farm lay in Kenley Road and became the centre for John Innes's farming experiments; in consequence it was always extremely well equipped. The dairy in particular was very successful and was eventually taken over by United Dairies in about 1926. It was converted into a bottling plant and remained in use until the late 1980s. It can be seen in the background to the left of the bus in the top photograph. (*George Hobbs*)

St Helier Avenue, 28 May 1952. Derby Day. Buses wait to be called forward to Morden Hall Road and from there summoned again to join the queue in Kenley Road. First in the queue is RT 64 which was added to the fleet on 29 February 1940. It usually worked around Putney but is having a day out taking racegoers to Epsom. The official London Transport schedule of duties required a total of 120 buses running at approximately one minute intervals. *(© Alan Cross)*

St Helier Avenue, 19 June 2005. A sign of the times that far more people now travel by car rather than bus. Whereas the buses were parked on the road, the cars are parked on what was the route of the original cycle path. Even in 1926, when St Helier Avenue was built, cycle paths were not new. The first dedicated cycle route was the Ocean Pathway opened in New York State in 1895 and said to be the oldest cycle path in existence. To accommodate the shared footpath/cycle path, the verge has been narrowed, but even so, the area is softened by more greenery than there was fifty years ago. *(George Hobbs)*

Morden Road, 20 April 1950. The roundabout junction with Morden Hall Road and Kenley Road is visible in the background in front of Hawes department store. At the end of the day, AEC Regent STL1636 is returning empty to its home garage after ferrying racegoers to and from Epsom Downs. STL stood for 'short type, long' (yes really!). STL buses were introduced when the maximum permitted length for two-axle buses was extended by a foot. Before 1932 ST (short type) buses had two axles and were 25ft long, while LT (long type) buses had three axles (see page 96) and were 26ft long. With devastating logic and a change in regulations, a two-axle 26ft bus became an STL – short type, long. The two passengers waiting at the bus stop on the opposite side of the road are *fascinated* by the photographer. *(© Alan Cross)*

Morden Road, 19 June 2005. Pelican crossings were introduced in 1969 and were themselves replaced by puffin crossings during the 1990s. Puffin crossings use sensors to detect the progress of traffic and should also monitor the movement of pedestrians to provide the optimum flow of both. Some work well but many merely ignore pedestrians and wait until there is a gap in the traffic; people grow tired of waiting and cross anyway. Hawes department store is now independent furniture store Wheatlands, the bus is new and the road is wider, but remarkably little has altered. We've even seen the bus before; it's the one pictured on page 94. *(George Hobbs)*

5

Time Off!

'Thomas Tew', 30 April 2005. Thomas Tew, a pirate with headquarters at Madagascar, had such a reputation for kindness that ships seldom resisted him. At least so the story goes. . . . The annual May Day event at Morden Hall Park in 2005 had a pirate theme, the star attraction of which was Bonny's Buccaneers, named after Anne Bonny, a notorious female pirate. During the event the Buccaneers delighted the crowd with demonstrations of authentic firepower. An historical re-enactment society, the Buccaneers are drawn from two other re-enactment societies, The Company of Ordinance [*sic*] and The Epyngham Retinue. 'Thomas Tew' is actually Colin Armstrong, Maître des Cannons (Company Master) of the Company of Ordinance. *(George Hobbs)*

Everyone has a different idea of fun (stop giggling at the back there!) and there is lots to do in Merton and Morden. For a busy suburban area there are plenty of green spaces thanks in part to the recognition by developers of their importance (see page 34). The Wandle was once a heavily industrial river, but industry no longer needs it either to power mills or remove waste, and it is now used mainly for recreation. The Wandle is deep enough for canoes, children paddle and fish in it and there are footpaths along its length where people can get away from traffic. One of the most attractive stretches of the river runs through Morden Hall Park, designed by Gilliat Hatfeild and now owned by the National Trust. The Wandle divides into a network of shallow streams running through a park that combines wetland, wide grassy areas, mature trees and a staggering array of plants and wildlife.

The river is home to many aquatic plants including bur reed, water crowfoot and water starwort. Hemlock water dropwort can also be found on the margins and the large, almost spherical flowers smell surprisingly pleasant, but the plant is highly poisonous. Watercress grows particularly well in the Wandle and, during the nineteenth and early twentieth century, was grown commercially and harvested from large artificial beds at Collier's Wood and Willow Lane. Increasing pollution ended the local watercress industry, although not all waste that ends up in the river is detrimental to the plant; Morden Hall Park, where watercress is particularly plentiful, is downstream of the Beddington Sewage Treatment Works!

As well as wetland, Morden Hall Park also contains old meadowland. It has not been ploughed for at least four centuries so is particularly rich in native flowers and grasses. Hatfeild introduced deer into his park in about 1870 and they remained until the Second World War. Morden Hall Park was then grazed by store cattle until 1972. Today the grassland is cut annually which allows plants to seed naturally. A greater variety of meadow plants can be found in the eastern part of the park as it has been relatively undisturbed. The western end of Morden Hall Park, near the level crossing over the tramline, is where some of the spoil was dumped from the digging of the Northern Line tunnel; another spoil dump was later landscaped and opened as Mostyn Gardens.

The tramline divides National Trust property, with Morden Hall Park on one side and Bunce's Meadow on the other. The latter is technically part of the park but doesn't appear to be so. Bunce's Meadow had previously been used as water meadow, calico bleaching ground, tip and allotments but now accommodates Deen City Farm. The Farm was founded in 1978 at Aberdeen Road in Mitcham – hence the name – and occupied a cramped site off Church Road from 1980. In October 1994 it moved to its current purpose-built premises in Merton. For some children it's their first introduction to farm animals and many volunteer to help out after school and at weekends.

Farms, green spaces and countryside were the norm for locals until the beginning of the twentieth century, so then entertainment took different forms. When the races were on in Epsom, families of gypsies made a 'hatching tan' or stopping place on Morden Common. The Romanies would hawk their wares from door to door in 'trushni' or baskets and local 'Gorgios' (non-Romanies) viewed them with suspicion.

Children, however, loved to watch the dark travellers and imagine an exotic lifestyle so far from their own.

Travelling entertainers visited Merton periodically and the space between the White Hart on Kingston Road and the railway line was used for performances. One entertainer who visited regularly had a dancing bear. He was Swiss and children nicknamed him 'Allez-en tenter' after the encouragement he sang to his bear as it danced. *Allez-en tenter* means 'Go on! Make an effort!' Dancing bears were outlawed in Britain in 1911, but the visits of the little Swiss ended some years earlier when the local policeman took him (and his bear) into custody. At least one former resident of Merton remembered the little man being understandably upset about the loss of his livelihood and his bear. He pleaded in broken English that the animal was well cared for and not dangerous. Locals wondered whether changes in the law concerning keeping dangerous animals were responsible. They never saw 'Allez-en tenter' or his bear again.

Only a few years later, in 1913, Merton's connection with the film industry began. J.H. Martin set up a film studio in Quintin Avenue where he produced a series of short films. One of his first in Merton was *The Mystic Mat* directed by Dave Aylott. The venture was run on a shoestring with totally unbelievable stories, jobbing actors and extras recruited from among the locals. Fictional film production only lasted about ten years initially. The studio was also used, however, by Publicity Films who made short filmed advertisements – a more subtle form of fiction perhaps. In 1928, with the advent of sound, Western Electric began making educational 'pictures' at Merton. During the 1930s and 1940s Merton Park Studios grew rapidly, until in the 1950s it was producing around sixty films per year.

All types of films were made at Merton Park, including documentaries, educational and advertising films and ones designed purely to entertain. Many famous actors spent some of their early career at the studio, including Michael Caine (*Solo for Sparrow*, 1962), John Le Mesurier (*Flat Two*, 1962), Bernard Lee (*Who was Maddox*, 1964) and John Thaw (*Dead Man's Chest*, 1965). The final film to be shot at Merton Park Studios was *Payment in Kind* in 1967. It starred Maxine Audley, Brian Haines and Justine Lord. The studios might have closed, but Merton's connection with filmed entertainment still remains as the ITV police soap opera *The Bill* is filmed locally; the photographer for this book has appeared in a crowd scene as an unofficial (and unpaid!) extra.

Entertainment may have changed but Merton and Morden still have a lot going on for residents and visitors alike to enjoy. And older forms of recreation have been rediscovered. The river is now one of the cleanest in the country. Busy shoppers hurrying from Merton High Street into the Savacentre cross the bridge over the Wandle, often within yards of fishermen dreaming over their rods.

Boxing booth, *c.* 1925. The tall man in the centre is John William Cotton, known as Jack, who lived at 157 Seymour Avenue and boxed under the name of Jack Williams. The house was later demolished by a flying bomb during the war; ironically, the only person killed in the explosion was a German gentleman living down the road who did not go to the shelter. The owner of the pavilion, Alf 'Spider' Stewart, ran a string of booths all over the country; this one was based at Croydon and made regular visits to Morden. The board outside the booth reads: 'Boxing by a well known troupe of boxers. Geoff Christian (USA) who

has fought three world champions including Jack Dempsey. Jack Stone of Manchester, Jack Williams of Burton on Trent, Jack Desmond of Johannesburg SA, Bill Driscoll of Wales, Frank Craig Soho son of the well known Coffee Cooler.' 'Spider' had six daughters and, as he had no son, taught them all to box. He made a lot of money as would-be champions thought that it would be easy to defeat 'mere' girls. His great-grandchildren are still fairground people today. Jack Cotton was a guardsman for a short time, but died at the tragically early age of 40. *(Derek Poulter)*

Outside broadcast, *c.* 1960. Mrs Jones was a teacher at Morden Farm County Secondary School but her husband was a commentator for the independent television channel which provided London's first weekday service. To the delight of the pupils, the school playing field was used for an outside broadcast. Unfortunately no one now seems to remember what was being filmed. Aragon Road is in the background. *(Derek Poulter)*

Outside broadcast, *c.* 1960. The door of the Bedford commercial vehicle is open so the legend on the side has been truncated. In full it reads 'Associated Rediffusion' (A-R) with, above it, A-R's logo or 'ident', the sixteen-pointed white star. A-R transmitted the first ever schools programme shown in the UK, so using school premises couldn't have been a novelty. The gymnasium of the old secondary school is in the background on the right. *(Derek Poulter)*

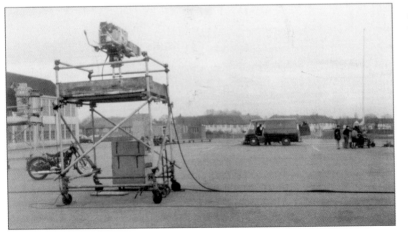

Outside broadcast, *c.* 1960. The same camera as above. Most programmes were still shown live; the picture was sent from the camera via the cabling to the temporary transmitter mast on the right and received in television sets and at the base studio. The school building on the left still stands and the row of houses in the background is Tudor Drive. *(Derek Poulter)*

Visit to *The Bill*, *c.* 2000. Merton and Morden are no strangers to filming and much of the action of the ITV police drama *The Bill* is filmed in the area. One employee at a local Merton firm turned up for work one day to find that the exterior of his office had been transformed into the entrance to a run-down block of flats and was surrounded by cameras. Not a lot of work got done that day! Pictured are Trudie Goodwin (left), who has played June Ackland since August 1983, and the Revd Sylvia Roberts, vicar of St John the Divine. *(Courtesy Church of St John the Divine)*

'St Hugh's Hospital, Canley', 22 May 2005. As the notice to the right of the picture indicates, this is actually Merton College transformed for filming an episode of *The Bill*. The action is taking place behind the notice to the right of the picture where the taxis are parked, but the photographer was not allowed any closer. For fans of the series, this particular scene appeared in episode 319, broadcast on Thursday 16 June 2005. PC 595 Tony Stamp, played by Graham Cole, was in hospital having been beaten up by local youths. Cole is noted in the series for insisting on doing all his own stunt work. *(George Hobbs)*

Sound Services Ltd film library, Wilton Crescent, *c.* 1965. Doris Walden is checking and splicing a repair to a film; one of the large reels is visible behind the lamp. Formed in 1936, Sound Services Ltd operated one of the largest sponsored 16mm film libraries in the UK. In 1964 the longest waiting list was for 'Coventry Cathedral', which was consecrated on 25 May 1962 and consequently Britain's newest cathedral at the time (see introduction to Chapter 3). Production of films at Merton Park Studios ceased in 1967 but the film library and projection services continued until the mid-1970s when they moved to Peterborough. *(E.P. Walden)*

Long Lodge, 267–9 Kingston Road, 6 August 2005. Built in 1746, Long Lodge is now home to the Bedford Insurance Group. In 1896 the building was owned and inhabited by the pre-Raphaelite painter Frederic Shields. When he died in 1911 it was purchased by John Brocklesby (see page 38), partly as a family home and partly for use as offices. In 1934 Publicity Films Ltd rented the offices and five years later the family left the area and the film company bought Long Lodge outright. *(George Hobbs)*

Summer fête, fund-raising stall run by 43F Squadron Air Training Corps, 1968. It sounds cruel now but the game of chance revolved around the hamster in the wire cage in the centre of the table. Hamsters inhabit semi-desert areas so the little animal shouldn't be too worried by the heat, but they are supposed to sleep during the day. Each box was numbered and contained a piece of lettuce. Once all the numbers were 'bought' the cage was lifted from the centre spot and the hamster released. Hamsters have very poor eyesight but excellent hearing and a keen sense of smell which would detect the lettuce. The 'owner' of whichever box 'Hammy' chose won a prize. Only girls appear to be taking part. Attracted by the cadets? Or the hamster? *(Courtesy 43F Squadron ATC)*

1st Morden Scout Group, Morden Hall Park, 30 April 2005. The tradition of young people raising money for charity continues. This time the game is curling, or rather kurling. Traditionally played on ice, in 2000 John Bennett invented the modern version – with a K – which can be played on any hard surface. Instead of granite stones sliding on ice Bennett's version uses discuses with a handle and small wheels. Currently played in forty-seven countries around the world, it's one of the few sports in which disabled people can compete against the able-bodied on equal terms. *(George Hobbs)*

Dart game, Morden Hall Park, *c.* 1967. The ATC regularly supports charity events. A letter dated 19 June 1967 addressed to Flt Lt Dixon from Sydney Astin, Hon. Secretary of the Merton & Morden Old People's Welfare Association, says: 'Your boys are to be complimented upon their appearance and for the ready way in which they performed all the tasks which they were asked to do . . . I am sure that you and your Cadets will be gratified to learn that there was a record attendance and that the nett profit will be in the region of £400.' A large sum in 1967. *(Courtesy 43F Squadron ATC)*

Bob the blacksmith, Morden Hall Park, 30 April 2005. Bob Oakes (right) of Cold Hanworth Forge and Blacksmithing School tours the country giving demonstrations and ad hoc lessons. Here he is teaching a member of the public how to make a paperknife. One of his demonstrations is to tie a knot in an iron bar. He says that it's exactly the same as tying a knot in a piece of ribbon except that you push instead of pull. He makes it *look* easy . . . *(George Hobbs)*

Victory in Europe (VE) day tea, the Green, Aragon Road, 1945. The girl nearest the camera in the centre is Eva Turner. The war in Europe officially ended on 7 May 1945 with the following day being declared a national holiday. Rationing was still on of course but women produced hoarded treats and queued at local shops for whatever food was available. To gain height the photographer rested the camera on the top of a telephone box; the curve of the roof is visible in the bottom left-hand corner. *(Courtesy Terry Walden)*

Silver Jubilee celebrations, the Green, Aragon Road, 1977. The phone box which played a central role in the VE day photography is visible in the background. The famous red telephone boxes were designed by Sir Giles Gilbert Scott to commemorate the Silver Jubilee of King George V in 1935. It is fitting that the K6 'Jubilee' model telephone box is still around to commemorate the jubilee of George V's granddaughter. This one was replaced by a stainless steel triangular model, but even that has been uprooted within the last two years, a victim of vandalism and mobile phones. *(Derek Poulter)*

Victory in Europe (VE) day party, the Green, Aragon Road, 1945. The man in the checked jacket is Herbert Scully, with the young man 'Sonny' Sharp to his left. Peter Daws is the boy in the ribbed jumper, while Brenda Baker is immediately to his left. The boy at the front in the centre is Terry Walden. The children have been instructed to 'hold up your mugs!'

They are 'Victory Mugs' made of white celluloid printed with a red and blue design. Memorial souvenirs are highly collectable now, particularly those not designed to be! *(Terry Walden)*

Victory in Europe (VE) day party, the Green, Aragon Road, 1945. First on the rope nearest the camera is 'Sonny' Sharp, while the boy with the light jumper behind Sonny's head is Terry Walden. The elderly woman in the centre is Ellen Wetherill, a visitor from Fulham, while the man on the right with the cigarette may be Frank Topp. The party was well organised and had a small stage with a backdrop of a large white V for victory. There was also a national dress competition; the girl in the Dutch costume in front of the V is Eva Turner. *(Terry Walden)*

Journeyman fletcher, Morden Hall Park, 30 April 2005. If the tug-of-war was known from the time of the Egyptians, the craft of fletching is even older. Originally used for hunting, arrows soon became one of the deadliest weapons of medieval warfare and the English longbowmen were feared throughout Europe. A skilled archer can fire up to fifteen arrows per minute with a range of more than 250 yards; from close range they can penetrate a 4in thick oak door. It is from archery that we get the rude two-fingered gesture. Before the battle of Agincourt in 1415 the French boasted that they'd capture the English archers and cut off the two fingers they used to draw the bow string. During the battle 10,000 French troops were killed at a cost of fewer than 200 English casualties. When the French finally conceded victory the archers who had won the day defiantly showed them their fingers. *(George Hobbs)*

AIR TRAINING CORPS

This is to certify that

Name *Dennis Alexander L. GODDARD*

Address *106 Marlow Drive N. Cheam Surr*

is a Member of the 43rd (MERTON & MORDEN) SQUADRON.

enrolled under the AIR TRAINING CORPS

.... (Name)

Date *1. 2. 41* 43rd (MERTON & MORDEN) SQUADRON (Rank)
Commanding

(SEE OVER) No.

Air Training Corps (ATC) enrolment card, 1941. The Air Defence Cadet Corps (ADCC) was formed in 1938 largely as the brainchild of Air Commodore J.A. Chamier. Each squadron's aim was to prepare their cadets for joining the RAF or Fleet Air Arm. When war broke out instructors were called up and cadets helped with much of the work on the ground. Realising the quality of the training cadets were receiving, the government took over control of the ADCC, instituted a number of changes and renamed the organisation the Air Training Corps. On 5 February 1941 the ATC was officially established, with King George VI as Air Commodore-in-Chief. Consequently, when Dennis Goddard joined the ATC on 1 February 1941 it did not officially exist! *(Courtesy 43F Squadron ATC)*

It is with a view to preparing myself for war-time serv
with either the Royal Air Force or the Fleet Air Arm or
Royal Navy (*cross out what does not apply*) that I am joining
the Air Training Corps.

I hereby solemnly promise on my honour to serve this Unit
loyally, and to be faithful to my obligations as a member
of the Air Training Corps.

I further promise to be a good Citizen, honouring my King,
my Country and its Flag.

D. Goddard
(*Signature.*)

43F (Merton & Morden) Squadron Air Training Corps, map reading class, 1964. These cadets are taking instruction from someone who had been on active service during the Second World War and had relied on his map-reading skills to survive. No wonder the cadets

are absorbed in what he has to say. Left to right are: Lance Corporal P. Davidson, Squadron Leader A. Doyle (RAF Retired), Cadets B. Davidson, G. Saker, C.J. Brown, M. O'Connell. *(Courtesy 43F Squadron ATC)*

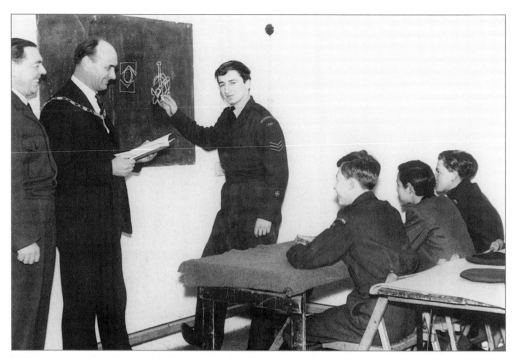

Visit by Councillor Vincent Talbot to the headquarters of 43F (Merton & Morden) Squadron Air Training Corps, 2 March 1965. Councillor Talbot was the Chairman of Merton and Morden Urban District Council – but only just. The last meeting of the Urban District Council was held that same month before Merton, Morden, Mitcham and Wimbledon became the London Borough of Merton. Standing, left to right, are Flying Officer J.J. Melican, Councillor Talbot and Cadet Sergeant Peter Davies. At the time the cadets were preparing to spend the following Sunday with the RAF for flying experience, and much of the evening was spent doing elementary parachute drill. *(Courtesy 43F Squadron ATC)*

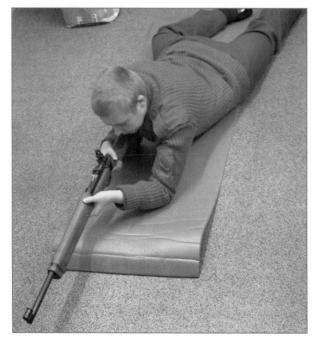

43F (Merton & Morden) Squadron Air Training Corps, 3 May 2005. The photographer had to be careful not to get in the way, not because the rifle was loaded with live ammunition (of course not outside a controlled rifle range), but because Cadet Penhale was undergoing an examination. He's demonstrating that he knows how to handle a bolt action No. 8 rifle, which is one of the two types of rifle used by air cadets. The other is the semi-automatic L98 but cadets are not allowed to use it until they become proficient with the No 8. Only when cadets prove that they can carry and handle a rifle safely are they allowed to fire it. Marksmanship can wait! *(George Hobbs)*

Cadets sanding down a wooden SE5a propeller, 1971. The SE5a was considered by many pilots to be the best British single-seat fighter of the First World War. After the war the biplane became popular as a sporting machine and was used for aerobatic demonstrations and aerial advertising. 43F Squadron inherited the prop from 350 (Carshalton & Wallington) Squadron in 1965. It is now mounted over the entrance to the lecture room and classroom in the squadron's headquarters. *(Courtesy 43F Squadron ATC)*

The SE5a propeller *in situ*, 3 May 2005. 43F Squadron Air Cadets meet at their headquarters on Tuesday and Thursday evenings. Earlier in the evening the cadets had been demonstrating their drill to a visiting senior officer on the parade ground outside. They are here listening to a talk on the theory of drill and being given tips to help them improve. Left to right are Corporal Sollis, Sergeant Hollness and Cadets Smith J., Gillmore, Burden, Aggett, Henry, Sawicki, Smith G. Despite appearances, girls are welcome to join the ATC; the lecturer, who is out of shot, was in fact female. *(George Hobbs)*

43F (Merton & Morden) Squadron Air Training Corps on a training course at RAF Swanton Morley, Norfolk, 1990. Swanton Morley was one of the airfields that mushroomed along the south coast and in East Anglia during the Second World War. First occupied in October 1940, it was used throughout the war mostly by Bomber Command. Swanton Morley only ever had grass runways so between 1957 and 1995 it

saw little RAF flying and was used for ground units and training. In 1996 the base was taken over by the Army. In true military style only surnames of the ATC cadets standing in front of the spitfire 'gate guardian' have been recorded. Back row, left to right: -?-, Head, Banks, Prangnell, Brown, -?-. Front row: Delrio, Berry, Marsham, Edwards, Brundle, Davis R., Cook. *(Courtesy 43F Squadron ATC)*

Cadet Sergeant Cook, 43F Squadron ATC, selling poppies, London Road, 13 November 1971. Remembrance Sunday is the one nearest to 11 November; it was 14 November that year. The trench warfare on the Western Front awoke dormant poppy seeds and carpeted the ground with scarlet. The blooms inspired the poem *In Flanders' Fields* written by John McCrae, a doctor serving in Flanders with the Canadian Armed Forces: 'In Flanders' fields the poppies blow / Between the crosses, row on row.' Since the Second World War there has only been one year, 1968, when no member of the British Services has been killed on active service. *(Courtesy 43F Squadron ATC)*

Cadet Carter, 43F Squadron ATC, selling poppies outside Caters supermarket, 13 November 1971. The first person to wear a poppy in remembrance was Moira Michael from Georgia. She bought some poppies, wore one and sold the others to raise money for ex-servicemen. The first official Royal British Legion Poppy Day was held in Britain on 11 November 1921. In 1922 Major George Howson formed the Disabled Society to help disabled ex-service personnel. Howson suggested that members of the society could make artificial poppies for sale and the Poppy Factory was founded in Richmond, London in 1922. It's still there. Seventy per cent of its workers are disabled or suffer from chronic illness and in 2005 they made around 35 million poppies. *(Courtesy 43F Squadron ATC)*

Taking the salute, entrance to Morden Park, Remembrance Day 1964. Previously wearing a bowler, as a civilian taking the salute Councillor Vincent Talbot, Chairman of Merton and Morden Urban District Council, quite correctly removes it. Leading 43F Squadron is Flying Officer J.J. Melican (saluting). The first cadet nearest the camera is Cadet Sergeant Peter Davies. Incidentally, the F after the number, stands for Founder; the squadrons thus named were the earliest to be formed. (*Courtesy 43F Squadron ATC*)

Morden Park, 10 July 2005. 43F (Merton & Morden) Squadron and 18F (Wimbledon) Squadron ATC parade to commemorate the sixtieth anniversary of VE/VJ Day. Veterans and ATC attended a memorial and thanksgiving service at Morden Park bandstand led by the Mayor of Merton's chaplain, the Revd Alison Price, Vicar of St Barnabas' Church, Mitcham. ATC members pictured are, left to right: Cadet Henry (43F Merton & Morden), Adult Warrant Officer Robert Smith (18F Wimbledon), Cadet Sergeant McHale (18F Wimbledon), Cadets Aggett (43F Merton & Morden), McHale (18F Wimbledon), Boyle (18F Wimbledon), Smith J. (43F Merton & Morden), Flight Lieutenant Ray Yee (43F Merton & Morden). (*George Hobbs*)

Excavation of Merton Priory, looking west, June 1988. The excavation was carried out by a team of archaeologists from the Museum of London. This part of the excavation revealed the foundations of the north side of the priory church. Merton Priory was cannibalised by Henry VIII to build his Palace of Nonsuch about 4 miles away. Demolition started even before the priory was officially surrendered and in all 3,600 tons of priory stone were reused. Most of this site is now underneath the Savacentre (see page 14). *(Courtesy Merton Abbey Primary School)*

Frieze inside the Savacentre, 6 August 2005. Leased and then owned by Edmund Littler, the mill specialised in accurate and detailed printed fabrics. By 1890 the Littler factory concentrated its entire resources on producing prints for Liberty; Arthur Liberty purchased it in 1904. Shortly before the First World War, Liberty decided to demolish Littler's old residence and, in doing so, discovered a late Norman arch (right in the picture above) incorporated within the building. The arch was thought to be part of the priory's hospitium or guest house. It was moved and reconstructed in the grounds of St Mary's Church where it can be seen today. *(George Hobbs)*

Excavation of the north transept, looking west, Merton Priory, June 1988. The north transept contained three side chapels each with its own altar. The building in the background on the left is part of the Liberty Mills complex. It was built in 1912 in two parts: the main building known as The Loft and a smaller building called The Cottage. In the 1980s its name was changed to The Showhouse when the building and its fellows were preserved and restored by the same team that developed Camden Lock. The area is now known as Merton Abbey Mills. *(Courtesy Merton Abbey Primary School)*

Merton Abbey Mills, looking north-east, 6 August 2005. The area is now an attractive blend of craft workshops, market, cafés and a local history display. The Showhouse is on the left with, next to it, the Colour House, a Grade II listed building. The latter was used for dying processes and is the oldest building on the site, dating from the eighteenth century. Some of the stone with which it is built may have been scavenged from the ruins of Merton Priory. The building on the right is Coles Shop and dates from 1890. It gets its name from Coles Print Works which was at Merton Abbey before moving to Hackbridge. Some of Coles' equipment was purchased and installed in the building. *(George Hobbs)*

Roy Scott, *c. 1970*. A member of the Radio Amateur's Old Timer's Association (RAOTA) and lifelong radio enthusiast, Roy lived at 140 Seymour Avenue. He is holding a spark gap transmitter. All radio hams were notified during the summer of 1939 that amateurs in possession of transmitting equipment should remove and pack all valves, and prepare an inventory of their apparatus so that a receipt could be issued for the equipment when collected. It may be that the intention was to return the equipment after the end of the Second World War, but this certainly didn't happen. During the evening of 31 August 1939 the BBC announced in its nine o'clock news bulletin that all amateur licences had been 'determined'. From then until the end of September, Post Office officials were engaged in impounding their equipment. Roy, however, joined a select group of secret listeners who had radio equipment returned to them in order to monitor and spy on enemy radio transmissions. One night during the blackout someone spotted the red light on Roy's radio receiver and reported suspected skulduggery to the police. They promptly arrested him! Only frantic and hush-hush telephone calls to Roy's 'control' secured his release, the return of his impounded equipment and the silence of the local force. *(Derek Poulter)*

Roy Scott's Radio Amateur's Old Timer's Association (RAOTA) car badge. A radio amateur can join RAOTA twenty-five years after being licensed. The year 1946 indicates when Roy first had his licence so the badge would be from around 1971. The main RAOTA emblem is an aerial (three arms at the top) and earth (series of horizontal lines) symbol with the letters RAOTA between the capacitor plates. The four small pictorial representations are, clockwise from top left: Morse key, headphones, thermionic valve (the symbol shown is a triode with inverted T as the anode, dotted line representing the grid and inverted U the cathode) and diode. G2CZH was Roy's call sign. *(Derek Poulter)*

Visit of Queen Elizabeth II to Wimbledon Broadway, June 1977. Mr Ives, Crossing Keeper for Merton Abbey Primary School, salutes the Queen as she passes with the Duke of Edinburgh. Pupils from the school are ranked behind him. During the celebratory year the Queen embarked on six tours in Great Britain and Northern Ireland, covering thirty-six counties. No other sovereign visited so much of Britain in the course of just three months. With tours to the Commonwealth, the Queen and the Duke of Edinburgh travelled an estimated 56,000 miles. *(Courtesy Merton Abbey Primary School)*

School tree notice. Merton Abbey Primary is good at planting trees (see page 49)! Pupils and teachers planted a silver birch for the school's silver jubilee in 1952 and Mr R. Davis planted another silver birch for the Queen's Silver Jubilee in 1977. During that year various species of trees could be ordered from the Borough Council and a record was kept of who had what; this tree is number twenty-four. Planting trees is appropriate for the school as classes in years 3–6 are named Elm, Pine, Ash and Oak respectively. *(Courtesy Merton Abbey Primary School)*

Opening of Merton Animal Hospital by Her Majesty Queen Elizabeth the Queen Mother, mid-1999. The Blue Cross hospital situated on Merton High Street replaced a smaller clinic on Penwith Road. Members of the local community spontaneously welcomed the royal visitor and Nathan Goodwin, a pupil at Merton Abbey Primary School, surprised everyone by his low bow. The Queen Mother was delighted! *(Courtesy The Blue Cross)*

ACKNOWLEDGEMENTS

Without the support, suggestions, help and photographic skills of my husband, George Hobbs, this book would not have been possible. I am also particularly grateful to Mr Alan Cross for the use of his historic photographs. Mr Cross is a professional photographer and without his generous help and support this book would have taken far longer to complete.

I should also like to thank the staff of Micro Anvika in the Whitgift Centre, Croydon, who managed to resurrect the text of this publication when the hard disk drive of my PC crashed and needed replacing. Without their help the book would have been at best very much delayed and at worst required much rewriting and re-keying.

Every effort has been made to locate all the copyright holders and obtain their permission to use the photographic material included in this publication. If there has been any error or omission in crediting the correct individuals or organisations the author can only apologise.

I am indebted to many organisations for their willingness to help with information and photographic material for this book. They include: 43F (Merton & Morden) Squadron Air Cadets, Ahmadiyya Muslim Community, Bishopsford Community School, The Blue Cross, The Church of St John the Divine, Emmanuel Church, Merton Abbey Primary School, Merton Park Primary School, The Sainsbury Archive and Sutton and East Surrey Water Company Ltd.

I should also like to thank the many individuals who rootled through their own or neighbours' lofts and cheerfully gave up their time to provide help, information and cups of tea. Many of them also allowed their photographs and other material to be reproduced. They include: Helen Brooker, R.M. Casserley, Alan Cross, Maxine Freshwater, Lilian Grumbridge, Paul Hughes, Joanna Jones, Mary Morris, Derek and Sue Poulter, the Revd Sylvia Roberts, Marion Talbot, Laura Taylor, Rosine Traisneau, Terence Walden and Flt Lt Ray Yee.

SELECTED BIBLIOGRAPHY

Much of the information for the captions in this book has been provided by the people who have loaned the photographs, but some has, of necessity, been derived from other documentation. The author acknowledges with gratitude the debt she owes to the following:

Anon, *Some Memories of Merton*, Merton Historical Society, 1983

Bayliss, Derek A., *Retracing the First Public Railway*, Living History Publications, 1981

Denbigh, Kathleen, *History and Heroes of Old Merton*, Charles Skilton Ltd, 1975

Edwards, Dennis, *London's Underground Suburbs*, Capital Transport, 2003

Forshaw, J.H. and Abercrombie, Patrick, *County of London Plan*, Macmillan and Co., 1943

Goodman, Judith, *Merton & Morden, a Pictorial History*, Phillimore, 1995

Hopkins, Peter (ed.), *St Martin's Church Morden: the First 40 Years 1957–1997*, St Martin's Church, 1997

Jowett, Evelyn M., *History of Merton and Morden*, Merton and Morden Festival of Britain Local Committee, 1951

Lawrence, David, *Underground Architecture*, Capital Transport, 1994

Leyden, Kevin, *A Historical Guide to Merton Abbey Mills*, Wandle Industrial Museum, 2000.

Livermore, T.L., *The Story of Morden and its Churches*, St Lawrence's Church, 1968

Merton Abbey Primary School, Log Book, unpublished

Mitchell, Vic and Smith, Keith, *Lines around Wimbledon*, Middleton Press, 1996

Seeley, Derek (ed.), *Merton Priory*, Museum of London Archaeology Service (MOLAS) and London Borough of Merton, 1993

Various, *The London Railway Record*, no. 24, Conner & Butler, 2000

Whichelow, Clive, *Pubs of Merton (Past and Present)*, Enigma Publishing, 2003

Yarham, Ian and others, *Nature Conservation in Merton*, London Ecology Unit, 1998